Breaking the Spiritual Care Code

Breaking the Spiritual Care Code

Toward a Standard of Practice

DENNIS E. KENNY

Foreword by
WAYNE MULLER

WIPF & STOCK · Eugene, Oregon

BREAKING THE SPIRITUAL CARE CODE
Toward a Standard of Practice

Wipf & Stock
An Imprint of Wipf and Stock Publishers
199 W. 8th Ave., Suite 3
Eugene, OR 97401

www.wipfandstock.com

PAPERBACK ISBN: 978-1-6667-6742-1
HARDCOVER ISBN: 978-1-6667-6743-8
EBOOK ISBN: 978-1-6667-6744-5

VERSION NUMBER 091323

To all those I have taught and who have taught me

Contents

Foreword

Why do we get sick? And if we do get sick, how do we heal?

These two questions—and our wildly diverse responses to them, across numberless centuries, cultures, ethnicities, and faith traditions—reveal a clear, unvarnished glimpse into our most basic beliefs about life itself.

Dr. Dennis Kenny, whose bona fides are prodigious, has worked for decades beside patients, collaborated with medical professionals, supervised chaplains, taught medical students, and helped guide countless spiritual care professionals in training. Here, his attentive work challenges the medical community to face a third critical question that demands fierce honesty and unblinking clarity.

If we ever hope to create, administer, or support a genuine, thriving healing community, we must confess our understanding of this third thing:

Do we focus our best care and attention on treating a disease—or do we perfect our most elegant, effective practices to heal the person presenting the illness?

Kenny suggests this is a false choice, a dichotomy of convenience. This too-common, binary approach allows medical, hospital, and administrative specialists to stay in the familiar comfort of their own lanes, rarely cross professional lines, and carve every patient's life into segmented areas of treatment. Sadly, the more we focus on categorically separate aspects of intervention in identifiable illness, we remain unnecessarily blind to a wealth of abundantly available, tender opportunities to harvest precious insight, collaborative wisdom, and often critical direction from the patients themselves.

Four of five hospital patients—when asked—will report having had a significant life loss within six months prior to their admission. Most patients—again, when asked—confess they feel "God has abandoned me," or "My illness is God's way of punishing me." Medical care ignorant of these two simple inner truths, vitally present in the minds, souls—and bodies—of these human beings they are seeking to heal, can make incomprehensible errors through a policy of willful institutional ignorance of these deeply essential, heart-shredding facts.

I have known Rev. Dr. Dennis Kenny for over twenty-five years as a colleague, collaborator, and—as often happens in creative, inspired and inspiring relationships with shared passion and vision—as a friend, someone who has been good company along this journey of illness and healing.

I use the word "company" intentionally, as I feel the quality of "good company" lies the heart of what Dennis is asking us to explore, illuminate, and prescribe for those who benefit from the gift of this work.

The word "company" is derived from *com-pan,* meaning "with bread." A companion, then, is "one who breaks bread with another." Dennis, sharing his vast experience in painful detail, narrates some of the deep sadness and confusion experienced by those who ache to be good company with patients in medical settings, as spiritual caregivers:

> *There are very few guidelines for how to do the job, which makes evaluating it difficult...[and] there are an amazing number of expectations. Spiritual caregiving is very broadly defined and occurs in a wide variety of situations. Burnout is high; caregivers search for ways to deal with expectations within themselves and from others.*

Some people we meet will be deeply religious; others, harmed or wounded by religion, want nothing at all to do with anything remotely "religious." And an enormous middle is populated with people everywhere in between.

Further, the percentage of people who describe themselves as "spiritual but not religious" has steadily risen for almost thirty years. So we all walk a razor's edge. How can any of us expect someone who is "spiritual but not religious" to accept us as a safe, trustworthy companion? At the same time, how can we ensure someone yearning for the comfort of an ordained leader in a specific, familiar tradition can find solace, knowing they are speaking with—or confessing to—a real priest?

Here, the depth and breadth of Dennis's experience allows him to offer a clear path for making sense of this complex, elusive role. I have seen him do this with students in CPE, in hospitals, and at the Institute for Health and Healing at CPMC, where we worked together for many years.

Above all, he teaches us to listen, clarify, challenge, and encourage. Spiritual care is not always about being the nice, listening, always supportive, vaguely "spiritual" presence. This role can feel safe, reliable, unproblematic. But we can be so "nice" we become emotionally bland, dishonest, and thoroughly unhelpful. In time, this "dishonest kindness" can become a significant factor in burnout, as we strive to offer kindness we neither feel nor honestly have to give.

Dr. Kenny defines spiritual care or holistic care in this way: "The discipline of focusing healing on the inner yearning or disease of the persons for whom we care." Sadly, precious few medical intake forms ask admitting patients about any of these basic human issues. What do they love, what gives them agency, what energizes, invigorates, resurrects them? If patients were asked that—if people were asked that—medical professionals could make strong, fiercely clear alliances with parts of their patients that are more alive, more whole, stronger, more fearless, willing to grow, heal, and live, and that abundantly.

As most institutional medicine ignores information about the person living with these inner conversations about loss, divine abandonment, or spiritual punishment, it is up to spiritual care professionals to fill in the missing pieces, to be good company.

If we agree that the inner lives of human beings—including their attitudes and choices around their life and work, their relationship with the Divine, with others, and themselves, all have a significant influence on whether they get sick or not, or can affect the progress of their healing—then our view of health care has to change. The importance of spiritual care in the prevention and treatment of people and their illnesses dramatically increases. It is no luxury, no comforting addition to "real" medical care.

Rather, as Dr. Kenny insists:

> *The trained and certified spiritual caregiver must speak as clearly and authoritatively as any other member of the health care team.*

Dennis Kenny's clear desire in sharing these experiences is "to understand more deeply, clearly, and honestly the value and impact of the critical role we play in the lives of people who suffer from both medical illness and spiritual dis-ease."

We can only thank him for this priceless, generous, inspired, and inspiring gift.

Rev. Wayne Muller, MDiv
New Mexico
May 2023

Preface

IN THE LAST SEVERAL years when I have looked for pastoral care or spiritual care books for courses I was teaching or for my own education, I have found books focused on care for specific groups of people or people in particular situations. Examples are titles like "Ministry to Cancer Patients or Heart Patients," or "Spiritual Care to Hospice Patients," or "New Approaches to Caring for Congregations," or those dealing with grief or trauma. These kinds of books have value and provide insight; however, the inference is that there is no standard of practice for spiritual care and that the spiritual care approach changes depending on the situation or the person being helped. While part of this is true, the risk is that spiritual caregivers are left without a foundational way to assess their work, make plans for their care, and communicate their work to other professionals in a consistent way. An exception to this is the work Edward Wimberly has done in describing pastoral care from an African American perspective. He writes of the importance of story and narrative and how it reflects the soul of the community. Carrie Doehring takes a system overview in her book *The Practice of Pastoral Care.*

My assumption and motivation for this book is that the guidelines for and approach to pastoral or spiritual care do not change from situation to situation.

In recent days important work has been presented by Christine Puchalski, Wendy Cadge, George Fitchett, Harold Koenig,

Ken Pargament, and others concentrating on the impact of care and researching its importance.

Clevenger and others talk of the need for greater education and base knowledge to develop the field and help those providing the care. "Without this base of foundational knowledge residents may leave CPE programs insufficiently prepared for the challenges they face in clinical settings such as how to meet the needs of diverse religious and non-religious populations."[1]

While more knowledge can be helpful, the comment misses the mark. It can send us on an endless search for more or correct knowledge, not unlike our approach in this country to medicine. Facts-based knowledge changes from case to case. What is needed is a standard of practice that teaches a system that can use knowledge and direct the relationship between the care provider and receiver.

Spiritual care has been seen as a singular activity influenced almost solely by the background and personality of the person providing the care. There is a sense that almost anyone can do it if they have a spiritual heart. What we have in common as to approach, evaluation, and communication of care has received little emphasis.

Megan Best, in two different journal articles on chaplaincy with palliative care and in the COVID-19 pandemic, has called for better education for spiritual care providers and a more defined code of practice. "Better education can help the healthcare practitioner to avoid being distracted by their own fears, prejudices and restraints and attend to the patient and his/her family."[2] In the second article she states:

> The critique that chaplains, unlike other healthcare professionals, are not subject to a shared code of conduct across healthcare specialities and institutions highlights the need for better advocacy efforts. The current state of affairs may impede the ability of chaplains to engage with healthcare and make it more difficult to be at the

1. Clevenger et al., "Education for Professional Chaplaincy," 223.
2. Best et al., "An EAPC White Paper," 9.

table when important decisions are being made about patient care during times of crisis or even in day-to-day management.[3]

The purpose of this book is to offer a way for people of all faiths or religious and spiritual approaches to identify and develop a system for understanding what it is we do; we need to *break the code for spiritual care and create a standard of practice* so that the system can be used by caregivers of all professional backgrounds and can be communicated using a common, clear language.

It was the July 4th weekend in the summer of 2022 and I was in Indianapolis at a national volleyball tournament where my two granddaughters, sixteen and fifteen, were playing. My wife and I had walked a long way from a concrete garage through a cold, mostly deserted hallway to get to the arena where the matches were going on. With over eight hundred teams the cacophony of sound was amazing as you walked in. Finding the court with the team you wanted to watch was a daunting task. We were successful and made it to our seats about ten minutes before game time. I turned to find my youngest granddaughter and then, I am told, collapsed and died. There were four MD's, one cardiac nurse, and an EMS chief on me in seconds. I felt the chief's healing touch on my chest for several weeks, and it was his face I saw and his words I heard when I regained consciousness. "Welcome back, bud." Now this is a story of miracles and of spiritual care.

I had a cardiac arrest, with no symptoms or physical concerns beforehand. It would be a couple of months before I learned why it happened, but I was told several times I was one of a very few survivors of this kind of physical event and "you were in the right place at the right time with the right people." The right people in this case being parents and fans of volleyball players, miracle one.

I spent seven days in the hospital over the July 4th weekend. Try to avoid going to the hospital over holidays.

I received great care during that stay from medical staff and students, nurses, and spiritual care providers. The director of the

3. Best et al., "A Long Way to Go," 46–48.

spiritual care department was a former student of mine, as was one of the staff chaplains. Director Trina Johnson walked in the first day and said to me and my wife, "I am here and I will stay here throughout this experience," and stay she did. Wayne Muller talks in the preface of "good company." I had it in many ways.

A surgeon was apparently eager to get me into his surgery suite for bypass surgery and came into my room looking patently disappointed and told me that he could not operate on me because I had several blood clots in the heart and he could not risk it.

I experienced spiritual caregivers with much experience and some with little, but they all seemed to share what I am writing about in this book. They seemed to know that it was not so much what they did for me but who they were for me. I felt the Holy in their presence.

I had many people from all over the country praying for me, notably the nuns who worked with my great friend Sr. Sheila Hammond. They prayed every day for me. My niece Dr. Darcy Lord, she of the PhD in holistic healing, put me on a list for twenty-four hours a day for a month for good intentions and healing thoughts. That does not count dozens of colleagues who sent notes and prayed.

Spiritual gifts came from many, including the chief of cardiology and his students. I asked him after they interviewed me if "I could ask them a few questions", and he gleefully agreed. The nurses brought hope with them every time they walked into the room. One told me as I was leaving, "We don't see many patients like you here." I remember being proud because I thought he meant I was doing so well and hadn't needed oxygen. He said, "Oh no, only about 5 percent of the people in your situation survive." There was a sense of urgency that each physician gave me as I left the hospital. I needed surgical intervention as soon as I could get it.

So back home outside of Chicago I saw several cardiologists and had many tests, waiting for a decision about surgery. After one test the cardiologist told me the blood clots had disappeared and that he had never seen anything like it. A chief surgeon told me I was the miracle guy and my heart was healing. He spent forty-five minutes with me and my wife, and we talked about prayer and things of the spirit as I did with each cardiologist I met. He said, "Oh yeah, I never mess with nuns." He shared his own physical challenges with us and closed with saying, "I am so glad we talked today." "Good companions," spiritual companions, come in all shapes and sizes and professions.

I was getting ready to play golf in late fall when the leading "expert" in cardiology in Chicago called me himself and shocked us by saying, "Well I've looked at all your latest tests and you're right, the blood clots are gone and your heart function is high normal, so there is no need for any intervention. You're good to go." What?! This was supposed to be a pre-surgery call.

In the following pages you will see companions sharing the things of the spirit. In their own way and time, they create miracles of healing as we all search for the mystery in the practice of spiritual care.

SECTION 1

Spiritual Care Assessment

1

Where Do I Focus?

IN MY EXPERIENCE AS a congregation's minister and as an Association for Clinical Pastoral Education (ACPE) certified educator and educator of psychotherapists, artists, administrators, doctors, nurses, congregational clergy, ministers, seminary students, and lay-people involved in ministry, one problem is apparent. Spiritual caregivers do not have a standard of practice to evaluate the work they do or find direction through the maze of expectations and issues that often accompany spiritual care. One of the major stressors of people who provide spiritual care full time is the lack of ways to measure success.

I believe spiritual care can be intentional and focused, professionally definable, communicable, researched, and respected. This book has been forged out of my own experiences in spiritual care and formed by those who have taught me and those whom I have taught. I offer it as a ministry to those who are interested in spiritual care, out of a belief that it can be more life-giving when we know why we do it, where we are going, and how we can get there.

Several years ago, the *Detroit Free Press* ran a series of articles regarding stress and burnout in religious and spiritual caregivers. The information was gathered through a survey of people involved in caregiving in the Detroit area. Its focus was on spiritual

3

caregivers in congregations, but the focus and pressures described fit caregiving wherever it takes place, as in hospitals, prisons, hospice.

Rabbi Daniel Schwartz of Temple Beth Emeth in Birmingham was quoted as saying, "People don't understand how stress filled this occupation is. You have a great many demands and a great many expectations, your own expectations, and others'. You can never meet those expectations."

The articles listed nine factors that seem to contribute to the reasons for burnout in religious and spiritual caregivers. At least six of them related to spiritual care situations and the confusion over knowing how to deal with them and how to evaluate when care was well done.

- *On stage, twenty-four-hour on-call responsibilities.* The minister of a United Methodist Church was quoted:

> In the last seven days, I have helped someone who ran out of money before their next paycheck, not really their fault; fed someone a meal; worked with a clergywoman on feeling the stress of a church expecting too much from her; worked with a woman in her sixties, recently divorced, never held a job in her life and now she is on her own; another woman in her seventies going through a divorce; talked with a woman in her early forties who has reentered the job market after divorce; and worked with a husband and wife separately about trying to reduce the stress within their marriage; all while helping to organize a youth retreat and an all ages church Halloween party.

In a conversation with a hospital chaplain, the content changed but the variety of demands was still there. She said, "It's been a rough few days. I cared for parents who had just lost their baby and I went back later and cared for the staff who had cared for them. I worked on my budget and had to figure out how to take 10 percent out of it. I helped organize a toys for families event for the holidays, and supported one of my staff chaplains whose mother was dying."

- *Nonstop emotional content.* With any spiritual care situation where people are cared for, the issues shared with the caregiver can be varied, deep, and legion. Compassion burnout is always a close companion. We've seen this acutely in the recent pandemic, where caregiving has often been overwhelming while trying to care from a distance and caring for families who often could not be near their loved one. Navigating these waters requires a sense of direction and assessment and intentioned response. Having someone near who is caring for the caregiver is essential.

- *Professional self-evaluation.* This was defined in the article as "Many clergy can't tell if they are doing their jobs well."

- *Keeping the peace between warring factions in a congregation or organization.*

- *The career trap.* Professional spiritual caregivers who have trained exclusively for that career sometimes wonder about their ability to compete in the secular job market. This has become more acute with dwindling congregation membership.

- *Loneliness.* Spiritual caregivers who do not feel themselves to be successful isolate themselves from peers and other professionals whom they see as more successful.[1]

There are several reasons for the isolation and burnout in spiritual caregiving or any caregiving for that matter. With full-time spiritual care providers, the above issues and demands are faced daily. For those who care for people spiritually on occasion or in the context of another role, the demands and complexity come up immediately when spiritual care is introduced as a part of general care. This is, in part, because since the beginning of time "one" has been set apart to speak to the Divine for the many. If you then decide to be a spiritual caregiver, clergy or not, the weight of the expectations and the challenges that go with the role will be felt. The confusion and difficulty in facing a variety of expectations

---

1. Seymour, "Clergy and Stress."

in a variety of situations, if there are no methods for selecting options or for measuring growth, become daunting.

Caregivers, no matter their profession, have a tendency to go with one style they were taught or found helped them or one that fits their skills. This boundaries all the caregiver needs to know and the choices of their response. The difficulty with choosing one style of caregiving is that people, their situations, and their needs change. What may be a good approach with one person may be very limited with another. The styles and the behaviors connected to them are not right or wrong in and of themselves. Used exclusively, however, they can become liabilities in the caring relationship.

So the answer to "where do I focus?" is on the varied needs of the person being served with as much freedom to respond as we can muster. The next chapter talks about some of the styles spiritual care providers use and their strengths and liabilities.

2

Caring Styles

The Listening Ear

IF A MINISTER HAS learned that the exclusive purpose of spiritual care is to listen carefully, the caregiver may follow that purpose regardless of the situation. The listening ear is a style that is very important and can leave people, particularly early in relationships, feeling cared for and appreciated. When the relationships go for any length of time, this style can very quickly wear thin. With people who are giving away responsibility to others for their life, caregivers who see themselves primarily as listeners may never stop hearing the litany of problems and hard times. People have no reason to consider their responsibilities for problems if they are not challenged or offered alternatives.

The spiritual caregiver who primarily defines ministry as good listening would generally not see calling to account as a part of their style. They would usually avoid any kind of judgment or directness in interactions with people.

Another style much like this is "being with" people. This style may leave the person to whom care is offered wondering whether the caregiver has any investment in them or opinions about their situation. It may leave the caregiver feeling unhelpful and useless because the issues they listen to and hear are not often brought to resolution in their presence or as a result of their interventions.

The Answer Person

My introduction to pastoral care in the seminary was in an "introduction to visiting" course. Our job was to spend a couple of hours each week at a hospital with a minister who, in a few short sentences, summarized his goals for his work. He had time to "find the problem and pray." He covered several hospitals and hundreds of patients. He would spend a couple of minutes talking to the person for the purpose of finding the problem and praying about it, then leaving for the next patient or hospital. There is a parallel with the charge nurse or administrator who understands their job as problem solving. Leaving a problem without solution feels unfair or uncaring. I remember clearly working with a COO of a prominent hospital who was a former marine. As I waited for him outside of his office for regular meetings, I would see people come out of the office in tears. He was an answer man and was brought to the hospital to find solutions. I learned quickly never to go into his office without solutions to any problems we discussed. Now, he wasn't offering spiritual care but he never deviated from his style, and people rarely felt heard or appreciated with him. It helped that I was raised by a Detroit cop and was less intimidated than some of my colleagues, and I made sure to keep his goals to find solutions at the forefront of our meetings.

The premise in this style is that spiritual care does not really flow out of the person of the spiritual caregiver or out of the relationship. It is based on the belief that care occurs in the sharing of theological or spiritual principles, scripture, prayer, or advice. It is a belief that the simple act of praying or reading from holy writings will take care of whatever problem is being shared.

Spiritual caregivers often feel burdened that they have to respond to every question asked and solve every problem presented. While that was true with the hospital administrator, it is not true in spiritual care. The major problem with this style is that the dialogue and the relationship are built around the questions asked or the problems presented rather than around the person to whom care is offered. The person often feels the caregiver does not want to be involved. They are often frustrated when questions they have asked for the purpose of giving voice to them are taken immediately to solutions they did not intend.

The assumption of the answer person is that once the question is framed or the problem is voiced then it becomes the property of the one giving the answers. The other assumption is that the person's inner resources are inadequate to cope with their questions and problems. The caregiver feels compelled to respond because it is expected and because they should have resources. Those with this style are burdened by everyone they counsel and may eventually feel overwhelmed when they discover that they cannot solve everything.

When people take the answer person's advice and suggestions and things end up failing, anger and hostility may be turned on the "poor spiritual caregiver" who does not understand why the person should be angry when all he or she tried to do was help.

The Exorcist

The exorcist style of care is based on a specific theological or spiritual approach which implies that problems, illness, or struggles are the result of sin or ill-advised behavior. The solution is to repent, and the problems will disappear. The "exorcist" promises quick fixes to complicated problems and blames the person's lack of faith if a cure does not occur immediately.

These caregivers are often judgers. There are many spiritual caregivers who are covert judgers, those who approach people with judgment but cloak it in niceness. The person receiving care ends up feeling awful but thinks that the spiritual caregiver seemed nice.

This style is based on a theological assumption that people are bad and do not have the theological resources within to help themselves.

The Cheerleader

The cheerleader style of care is typified by the phrase "let's look on the bright side." In the face of whatever problems people present, the response is usually along the same lines. I've heard conversations go something like the following:

The caregiver asks, "How are you today?"

The patient responds, "Well, not so good."

The caregiver smiles and says, "At least the sun is shining today and you can enjoy that."

"It's hard to enjoy life when you're in the hospital," the person says.

The caregiver quickly asks, "Has your family been to see you lately?"

"Yes, they have," answers the patient.

"Well, I am sure that was very helpful and supportive for you."

The patient responds, "Well, no it wasn't. My wife was angry and said if I had taken better care of myself we all wouldn't be in so much difficulty."

The conversation continues along these lines or ends very abruptly with the caregiver being asked to leave.

The person receiving care may never be aware of the lack of connection. They may feel discounted and uncared for because their feelings were ignored. Spiritual caregivers in this situation are very often frightened and uncertain of their own competence in the face of difficult questions. They put undue pressure on themselves to answer questions that often have no answers. When presented with these situations, they often change the subject. The cheerleader often stays away from people who are in crisis.

It is out of personal and observed experience with the above frustrations and a desire for direction and a standard of practice that this book is born. Spiritual caregiving can be enriching and freeing rather than debilitating and limiting. I believe it ought to be in response to others' needs. It should come out of an awareness of our own needs with knowledge of the boundaries of our strengths and limitations. Its origins and resources rest in our relationship with God or the Divine, however we define the Other in our lives.

Spiritual care assessment has never been easy for caregivers. It has been difficult because those who do the work are often reluctant to judge people and their dynamics. Spiritual caregivers may believe their responses will stay the same no matter what the assessment.

In the first place, all of us make judgments and assumptions about people and their behavior. We make decisions based on theological or other worldview assumptions that guide our responses. The intent of this section is to present a framework that will help bring those assumptions to light, evaluate them, and change them if necessary.

In the previous examples, the caregivers take one approach, which may arise out of their own unmet personal needs or unexamined theological or spiritual approaches to people. Those who carry one style into all the situations they encounter will frustrate themselves or the persons for whom they care.

Spiritual caregivers with limited choices usually respond by avoiding behavior they have difficulty with, what they try to stay away from. They may have a difficult time helping people come to judgment when they have trouble with judgment themselves. They may place an overemphasis on answering questions or doing for others when they are searching for answers themselves. There are occasions when we can do for people, problem solve with them and be successful, but if we are afraid to face certain issues or feel we don't have the resources to deal with them, then over the long run quick solutions fade and we open ourselves to burnout and depression.

Burnout in spiritual caregivers these days is at a crisis stage and not just because of the virus of 2020. In the above examples, *it comes from taking too much responsibility or too little*, thus limiting our responses. Choosing one style does ease the pressure on us, because it saves us from doing assessments and thinking through responses and pushing us to know our field and use our knowledge to assess and respond. I see it in well-intentioned caregivers who have decided that above all else they need to be considered "nice" people. This is difficult to do, with the demands and expectations of caring for others. If the intention is to be nice and not offend anyone, trouble arises because people are different and their expectations of the caregiver differ.

What can help is a standard of practice that includes a system of assessment that guides us through the maze of situations we face, that encourages a range of responses and gives us a framework that can help us focus our care.

The next chapter begins that process with the definitions for the work and an introduction to spiritual assessment.

3

Definitions

A DEFINITION FOR SPIRITUAL care or holistic care is as follows:

The discipline of focusing healing on the inner yearning or dis-ease of the persons for whom we care.

This definition emerged during the period I helped lead the Institute for Health and Healing in San Francisco, which became the largest integrative medicine program in a hospital in the country. We were working to define our task in a very traditional medical center. Our mission was to try and bring the person receiving care into the center of treatment rather than having the treatment and those providing it be the major focus.

Going back almost sixty years, Rev. Carroll Wise did the same thing. In a time when stock prescriptions from clergy were the norm for helping people, Wise and others writing in the late 1920s and 1930s talked about putting the needs of people at the center of care. This caused the caregiver to frame their responses by the dynamics and needs of the person receiving the care.

Wise's definition is in his book *The Meaning of Pastoral Care*: "*Ministry is bringing the 'Good News' to the point of people's needs.*"[1]

---

1. Wise, *Meaning of Pastoral Care*, 8, my emphasis.

These definitions then require an assessment (finding people's needs, their yearning or dis-ease) and a response focused on the needs or dis-ease.

Based on these definitions, the care has a much greater chance of having direction and a system of evaluation that ultimately can lead to greater sensitivity to people and their needs.

Out of these definitions, two questions need to be addressed as a part of the discussion of spiritual care assessment.

a. What is the effect of inner turmoil and disruption on people's illness, wellness, and recovery?

b. Are there specific religious needs that caregivers can identify as a part of their assessment, that set spiritual caregivers apart from other disciplines and help define their caring?

The answers to these questions are reflective of the biases in this book. Answering the questions goes a long way toward defining how spiritual caregivers react to other disciplines and how they define their place and role in relationship to those disciplines.

What is the effect of inner yearning and turmoil and disruption, or dis-ease, on people's illness, health, and recovery?

Although the impact of emotions on illness is much talked about, it is an issue that is getting very little attention in medical schools. The exception appears to be some family practice curricula. In my experience it is a topic that is looked upon with great suspicion by physicians, even though they may consider themselves "holistic" in their approach.

I co-led a course for medical and surgical house officers in a residency training program called "Emotional and Spiritual Issues in Illness." The attendance significantly decreased as we began to discuss these issues, even though we made sure they got lunch during the seminars. The house officers present asked time and time again if there was research to back up some of the points of view presented. When we brought the research to them, they were very reluctant to trust the studies and accept the findings. They were much more concerned with diagnosis and treatment than the prevention and etiology of illness. The house officers I worked with saw this discussion as patently nonscientific.

Patients also have difficulty dealing with their role in being ill. If they see they have had a hand in creating their situations, it is sometimes difficult for them to face. Do people's emotions and the way they care for their inner worlds affect their relationships and physical selves?

About six months before my father was to retire, he came down with a mysterious virus and was hospitalized. For the next nine months he was in and out of the hospital but increasingly more ill, to the point where he was placed on a respirator and we were sure he was going to die.

During that time, I made several trips to the hospital to see him. I saw several of his colleagues while they visited him. Out of the six people I saw, all were due to retire within the next year or two, and all save one were scheduled for some sort of serious surgery or had been seriously ill within the last year. The exception was a man whose wife had just gone into the hospital for coronary by-pass surgery.

In a conversation with one of my father's friends, we mutually agreed there were much better ways to retire than to become ill. Our story had a happy ending: The respirator assist was enough to help my father's system fight the virus, and he did recover. About a month or so after his last hospitalization, we received word they had identified the Legionnaires' virus as the problem.

In informal surveys at a large metropolitan general hospital and a state psychiatric hospital, one hundred patients were surveyed at random and asked, "Has there been a significant grief experience six months prior to your hospitalization?" Over 80 percent responded affirmatively.

Anyone who has provided spiritual care for any length of time has heard many stories of people who have followed grieving or times of high stress or other significant life events with illness. For those of us who see people in these situations and try to help them, this connection is not surprising news.

"The Stress Test," the life situations questionnaire developed by psychologists Holmes and Rahe, which assigns points for stress events in people's lives, has even been accepted by insurance companies as information for their clients. The higher the point value on the scale, the more likely the person is to get sick.[2]

In a large study by Dr. Harold Koenig and Dr. Ken Pargament Using the religious coping index (RCOPE) and the brief RCOPE, the researchers found that the negative questions about one's relationship with the Divine and their illness indicated serious challenges to a person's health when answered in the affirmative. "The Negative Religious Coping" subscale has emerged as a robust predictor of health-related outcomes. The four items on the scale that had the most health impact were "felt God has abandoned me," "felt punished by God," "wondered what I did for God to punish me," and "questioned God's love for me."[3]

What are the implications for spiritual care? The first and most important implication is that if we agree that a person's attitudes, reactions and choices concerning their work, their relationship with the Divine, with others and themselves; influence whether they get sick or not or can affect their healing then our views of health care must change. The importance of spiritual care in the prevention and treatment of people and their illnesses dramatically increases.

What are the implications for health care if this philosophy is accepted? The person and their approach to life needs to become an important factor in diagnosis and treatment. It changes the exclusive focus on physical diagnosis and treatment that is so much a part of modern health care treatment. Such a change would radically alter the way we train and educate medical doctors in this country. It would reorganize the priorities for budgets and programs for health centers and hospitals. The bottom line of this whole point of view is that we would need to begin to look at *disease* in people's lives rather than only at disease.

2. Rahe et al., "Stress and Coping Inventory," 199–208.
3. Pargament et al., "Brief RCOPE," 51–76.

The implications for the ill person may lead to a variety of emotional reactions at having to consider whether one's life choices have impacted our being ill. The frightening part may be, "Oh no! I've given myself something and now I feel worse!" Another possible reaction may be, "I'm sick, I have some ideas why. At the very least I can put things in order in my life to bring the best resources I can to cope with my illness, resources I didn't even know I had."

People who are ill can find out that they are participating in their illness and thus can become vital participants in their return to health. It empowers people not only to deal with the stresses, strains, and dis-ease in their lives but also to cope with the many decisions that are required of them as patients.

The implication for the spiritual caregiver is that the trained and certified spiritual caregiver can speak as clearly and authoritatively as any other member of the health care team. The caregiver can begin to be an assessor of people's dynamics. Congregations and religious or spiritual groups can become major participants in the wellness movement in our country. They can continue to be what they have always sought to be, bearers of peace and comfort. Spiritual caregivers who do not accept the premise that people are participants in the state of their health will continue to be spectators and passive recipients of an increasingly mechanistic health care system.

Spiritual caregivers are often seen as a first line of defense in people's struggles with life. The leaders of spiritual and religious groups are often people to whom someone comes when there is a crisis. Because of this, the caregivers are uniquely suited to aid people in coping with situations in their lives in healthy ways and helping them avoid choices that lead to illness as a coping mechanism with life's difficulties.

Circumstances or events in life can cause disruption in people's understanding of themselves and their world and their needs. If not handled in healthy ways, these events can be a major contributor in dis-ease or unhealthy behavior. When people struggle with stressors in their lives and don't do it very well, then the genetic and or environmental predisposition for illness comes into play and can assert itself more strongly.

We are not doomed to being ill when significant events happen to us, but it is the relationship between our resources for coping, the strength of the trauma or the critical situation, and the support systems that we have gathered around us that can affect the way we cope with these life situations. When the events and circumstances in our lives overwhelm our coping resources or our support systems, then we are much more likely to become ill.

Understanding health and illness in this way returns a person's power, puts the individual at the center of what is happening to them, and places the spiritual caregiver in a vitally important role in caring for people.

4

The Task of Spiritual Assessment

ARE THERE SPECIFIC RELIGIOUS *needs that define the spiritual care-giver's task and set them apart from other disciplines?*

In health care settings these days, this has become an important question. Budget restraints and cutbacks have become commonplace. Disciplines wishing to retain their budgets are working hard to define the uniqueness of their function. There is a lot of interest in protecting turf. Over the years spiritual caregivers and others have defined spiritual care as "responding to religious or spiritual issues." The question here is "are there religious or spiritual issues?"

There was a time in the development of the pastoral care function in Christian ministry when ministers could not describe theologically what they did. Paul Pruyser, writing in the 1970s in *The Minister as Diagnostician*, indicates that during training for ministers at the Menninger Clinic the ministers had a difficult time defining people's issues from a theological point of view. They could use psychological and family systems and other language but stalled when asked to describe dynamics in theological or spiritual terms.[1]

It is natural for ministers to want to be able to define their role and the issues that belong to them. It helps their image of

1. Pruyser, *Minister as Diagnostician*, 24.

themselves and helps define their role for other people. It also helps them say what it is they don't do. It can be attractive to hear someone from another discipline say, "I don't deal with religious things. You take this part of the person's struggle." It is attractive because it appears to clearly define our role. It appears easier, but I don't believe in the long run that it is helpful to the spiritual care provider or the person receiving the care.

I don't believe that there are religious or spiritual needs that uniquely define the role of the spiritual caregiver. I believe that there are people with specific approaches to life and with basic life needs who experience dis-ease or unmet yearning when buffeted by life events. The task of the spiritual care assessor is not to look for religious or spiritual needs but to look for dis-ease or yearning and name it theologically or spiritually. Describing what is happening to people in our vocabulary and from our perspective is what sets us apart and what sets any profession apart.

Each discipline views people and their concerns from their specific vocabulary, their worldview, and their uniqueness. It should be no different for the spiritual caregiver.

This multidisciplinary thinking allows a variety of professionals to interact as a team to coordinate a response appropriate to the person and his or her illness. This approach can put the person being cared for at the center of the assessment and treatment. They then can choose the discipline or definition of the problem with which she or he is most comfortable. This approach came alive at the Institute for Health and Healing at California Pacific Medical Center in San Francisco. When a person came into our Integrative Medicine Clinic, we listened to them and let them choose how they wanted to be treated. It was required, if their illness was serious enough, that they had seen a primary care physician for diagnosis and suggested treatment. Our desire was to team with their MD and create an integrated care plan. Our team included MDs, a wide array of body workers, spiritual care providers, psychotherapists, and others. We had one approach in common and we hired for it. We wanted people on the team who considered themselves healers and who treated the whole person. It didn't matter the discipline; each voice mattered and shared their approach to the healing and wellness of the person we were seeing.

This approach places the health care spiritual care provider in a significant role on the health care team. It offers spiritual care providers of all faiths and beliefs new ways of relating with people to whom referrals are made. It places their wealth of experience and their expertise with people at a key spot in people's wellness and recovery. It places the person needing help with a variety of options and people to choose from on their journey to health and healing.

We were committed to helping people no matter their life circumstances, spirituality, gender, culture or race, insurance or financial resources. People came to us for health enhancement, for supportive care to serious illnesses, and for alternative approaches to care they had received.

Beth came into our clinic with a serious breast cancer diagnosis and a desire to not just treat it traditionally. She had assessed her physical issues as coming from the way she worked her job. She had made work her highest priority and not relationships. She saw her problem as a spiritual one, and she wanted nutritional advice and body work to get back in touch physically. She had begun plans to move to India and live in an ashram in order to meet her spiritual goals.

She first met with the team to share her views and see what we could offer her. We suggested as a first step that she meet with one of our MDs who was trained as an oncologist and a nutritionist.

We wanted to respect her values, respond to her fears and hopes for healing. After counsel with the doctor she decided to go with a modified plan rather than the one suggested by her surgeon. She agreed to a lumpectomy and radiation and then returned to us for other treatment. She selected the nutritionist, a body worker who was prized for her compassion and sessions, with me to look at the spiritual side of her illness.

This was a woman with obvious resources in a city with an endless supply of caregivers. She could afford to leave her job and go to India for a year. She was determined to change her life and defeat the illness.

She and I talked about the need to change her life and connect more directly with her emerging spirituality, She knew she had a serious illness and thought she needed to take serious action. She acted on her plan to go to India and did live in an ashram for a year, daily following spiritual practices that were a part of that community.

The good news is that she is healthy several years later. She is still following her spiritual practices faithfully. She now has a job she loves and that allows her to breathe.

Susan came to us complaining of food addiction, depression, and spiritual distress. She brought five typed pages of prescriptions with her to her first team meeting. She was not happy. We devised a plan with her to meet with one of our MDs who was a nutritionist, as well as with our acupuncturist, and with me as her "spiritual advisor." In addition, she kept in touch with another MD who was a psychoanalyst. Susan had very few resources. We worked out a payment and some exchange of services plan. She relaxed and made good use of her time.

Susan's work with me consisted of talking about her very conservative Catholic upbringing and the negative self-image that had come out of her childhood. She believed that was what had led to her significant weight gain and several failed relationships. As we talked over several weeks, it became clear that she had suffered sexual and physical abuse at the hands of family members. She had attached spiritual and religious messages to these experiences. She began a journey of religious and spiritual reeducation and different life choices. She used several members of the team to work on these issues from different perspectives. My relationship with her was focused on understanding her spiritual and religious principles in new and more life-giving ways.

Addressing these two questions brings us back to the two principles that undergird the discussion of spiritual care assessment in this book.

First, there are circumstances and events that cause dis-ease or effect yearnings in people's understanding of their life, i.e., their orientation to themselves, to their relationships, and to God or Holy Other. When these disruptions don't receive attention, they may affect healing, lead to illness and unhealthy behavior.

Second, the task for the spiritual care provider is to assess the person's type or worldview and which needs are dis-eased or which yearnings need attention and name them theologically or spiritually.

The task of finding and defining is natural for the minister or spiritual caregiver because, more than any other profession, we are trained and oriented to judge right and wrong and to recognize good and evil.

One afternoon I received a surprise call from the publicity department at the Cleveland Clinic asking if I'd appear on a panel at a clinical lawyer conference. The caller explained that, much like we did in clinical pastoral education with spiritual care providers, they oversaw the work of legal students in community clinics. The audience was particularly interested in how to help these developing professionals set boundaries with the people coming to them for help. I learned that day that we did have a lot in common, and I liked them as a group. They were committed to helping people without resources and educating students to do the same. On the panel that afternoon sat a Harvard professor, a Georgetown professor, and an author who had written extensively about community clinics. We were asked as a panel to respond to a question about how to help the students set boundaries with clients. One example was that one student had invited a financially stressed client to come live with them. The group had a variety of suggestions on how to offer lectures, role play, case studies, and other approaches. One member of the audience addressed the question to me, asking how as a minister I would respond and how I got students to do what I wanted. After a thoughtful pause I said, "I tell them if they don't do it then they're going to hell." There was a stunned pause following that answer, and then significant laughter broke out (fortunately). It seemed that clinical lawyers, much like ministers, often feel that it is inappropriate to judge or categorize or put people in boxes because it limits them or is not loving.

The difficulty is not judging or categorizing people; rather the difficulty arises when we do not bring our judgments under scrutiny and use them to help us understand the world of the people we serve.

Spiritual caregivers tend to believe that if they love and listen to people, that is a sufficient definition for a spiritual care situation. It is as if listening and loving look the same and are received the same for all people in all situations. How we listen, how we love are questions that arise naturally and need to be guided by an assessment process.

Spiritual care providers need a definition of care that allows an assessment process and a response process that flows from the assessment. To focus on either assessment or response exclusive of the other limits the care.

A definition of care that only focuses on assessment is primarily an information-gathering function that risks treating people as objects, i.e., "the job of care is to find where people have gone astray." A definition that focuses on response runs the risk of responding to every person in the same way regardless of his or her situation, i.e., "the task of spiritual care is to love and be with people."

The concern many professional spiritual caregivers and other professionals have about ministers making assessments is the fear that a judgment will be imposed. For example, a minister assesses that distress in a person's life is caused by the sin occurring there and berates the person for being a sinner or just focuses on the sin and the need for forgiveness. The concern is only valid when the definition of care stops at the assessment or uses the assessment without sensitivity to the person and his or her needs.

Spiritual care assessment prepares us to respond, gives us direction and goals for response. It is not in itself the response. It can inform our responses, but it does not make our responses insensitive to the world of those receiving care. In fact, its purpose is to make our responses more sensitive to the needs of people.

Historically, other disciplines have feared that ministers would impose their own biases and theologies without concern for the particular worldview of people they serve. This is one of the reasons for the rise of people describing themselves as spiritual versus religious. If spiritual care providers are to communicate confidence about their role to other disciplines, it is important for them to be clear that assessment does not function on its own. It only serves an informed, sensitive spiritual care response.

Diagnosis is a term that has been associated with medicine and medical care over the years. It is often understood to be a word that definitively states the parameters of a person's situation. This kind of assessment is seen as limiting people's freedom and is why some spiritual caregivers balk at being diagnosticians. It does not seem to fit with what they are called to do when they assess.

The word diagnosis has its root in the Greek word *gnosis*. One of its primary meanings is "to know with a certainty or the finality of an emperor."[2] Christian Scripture has another word that more accurately reflects the act of assessment. The word in Greek (spelled phonetically in English) is *diacrisis*. It is a word meaning "to distinguish, to judge, to separate out." In 1 Cor 12:10, for example, the word is used to describe an "ability to distinguish between spirits." Hebrews 5:14 refers to an ability to differentiate good from evil.[3]

Spiritual care assessment, then, is the process by which providers can distinguish between spirits in the life of a person to inform the relationship of care.

It is essential for spiritual care providers to be diacritics if they are to have a way to evaluate and to set goals for their care. Diacrisis is essential in spiritual care whether or not providers see themselves as being the main caregiver.

Diacrisis or spiritual care assessment is a thinking, intentional, and structured way to look at people and their needs. Spiritual care response is caring for people within a relationship guided by that assessment.

2. Mounce, *Analytical Lexicon*, 128.
3. Mounce, *Analytical Lexicon*, 139.

Section 1: Spiritual Care Assessment

Spiritual care assessment, then, has three tasks:

a. Describing the care receiver, their type (the way they are in the world)

b. Finding the needs that are yearned for or have become dis-eased

c. Naming those needs areas spiritually or theologically

5

Types and Needs

Listen to the voices of longing in your soul, listen to your hungers.
Give attention to the unexpected that lives around the rim of your life.
Listen to your memory and to the onrush of your future, to the voices
of those near you and those you have lost. Out of all that, make a prayer
that is big enough for your wild soul.[1]

JOHN O'DONOHUE

THERE ARE A LOT of typologies that describe people and their dynamics: Myers-Briggs, Enneagram, and on and on. All, it seems to me, can be helpful in identifying the type of person we are dealing with and how we might best help them.

There are systems that start with identifying needs rather than identifying the kind of person. I start with the type of person because, even with the same needs, different people respond differently depending on their default type or their way of looking at the world, while they make a prayer with their living that is unique to them.

---

1. O'Donohue, *Eternal Echoes*, 220.

I have for most of my life tried to understand people in the simplest way I can. This is probably because this reductionist way of thinking helps me feel like I can actually understand the complexity of my life and that of others. While this may be delusional, it has helped me and others while in the middle of a crisis feel that there might be light at the end of the tunnel.

Types

I have found that there are three types of people with need areas that are yearned for and get distressed and dis-eased.

a. The first is Achievers. Putting work and success over the ability to build relationships, to give and receive love, to love and empower others, their need area centers around taking *responsibility*.

b. The second is the Giver. These are people whose need for *worth* is lodged in helping others. They put others' needs and desires above their own.

c. The third type is the Searcher. They are people whose need centers around their yearning for meaning and purpose in life. They need a *commitment* outside of themselves that gives life meaning.

It is not always easy to decide which is the primary type or primary need. Types and needs are distinct, however, and it is helpful to choose a type or need area as the primary focus. Each calls for a very different response from the spiritual care provider.

Each person has all three areas of yearning and need. A healthy dose of each makes a healthy person. While that is true, each of us has a default primary need that asserts itself when we are challenged or in crisis. Many experiences in life bruise and batter our sense of self-worth, our abilities for responsibility in loving relationships, and our ability to commit to meaning outside of ourselves. The coping abilities that the normally healthy person has are usually adequate to adjust to these experiences.

However, when we have multiple or severe emotional traumas or crises, life can keep us from what we yearn for or create dis-ease in one or more of our need areas. Though dis-ease may occur in more than one area, I believe that there is a primary diseased or affected area in each situation for each person.

Much like our physical selves react in crisis, we have emotional and spiritual predispositions for dis-ease as well. Persons who have had their sense of self and their ability to give damaged tend to blame themselves in crisis. People who place achievement first and experience roadblocks to their goals blame others. Searchers get lost in crisis, don't know who to blame, or choose a neutral stance.

Each person's primary type and need has its own "symptoms" and "prescribed treatment." Much like a doctor would not treat a cataract with chemotherapy or a kidney stone with an elastic bandage, spiritual care providers ought not respond to one type of person with the responses appropriate for another.

People and their needs are very different in character; they yearn differently and get dis-eased differently. They call for different responses.

Needs

Many years ago, Howard Clinebell in his book *Basic Types of Pastoral Care and Counseling* drew a distinction between presenting issues or short-term issues and longer-term or core issues as he talked about whether short-term counseling or longer in-depth counseling is called for.[2] That distinction has stayed with me as I've tried to understand where to begin in a caring relationship and where to focus. The spiritual care provider's task is to keep one eye on the presenting issues and one on the core issues. This is true when the presenting issue is so big or emergent that it demands attention. The reason is that understanding a person's type, which in my definition means the way they are in the world and in

2. Clinebell, *Basic Types of Pastoral Care*, 114–15.

their relationships, will change *how we respond* to their presenting issues.

With the variety of issues that come to any person caring for others, it is not an easy task to distinguish between what is "core" and what is presenting. Who they are and how their identity has been formed frames how they are in the world and where their yearning and needs reside. It is not easy to distinguish between presenting issues and the core type and needs, but it is vitally important. By needs, I mean people's basic emotional or spiritual orientation to themselves, their relationships, their world, and God/the Divine. It is within these needs that yearning is held and dis-ease takes place. The needs of *responsibility, worth*, and *commitment* are where spiritual care needs to be focused.

Following a workshop I did on "assessment in spiritual care," a Christian minister said to me, "You know, after several years in parish ministry, I now understand why I sometimes feel like I am going in circles or putting out bush fires. I have never quite been on target in terms of how people view the world or what they need. There always seems to be something lurking in the background that needs my attention, but the issues in the foreground keep demanding that I do something with them."

There are times when we have no choice but to respond to what is right in front of us because of its significance. I am not advocating that we ever ignore or discount the intense grief of someone who has just lost a loved one. We dare not ignore a threatened suicide or a physical crisis. It can make a difference, however, if we try at the same time to do some assessment of the impact of these events on how people view themselves, other people, or their purpose in life.

Take, for example, a person who enters the hospital for surgery. The patient's spiritual caregiver makes a pre-surgery visit and the nurse voices concern that the patient is very anxious and afraid.

In one possible scenario the caregiver sets a goal to help the patient get fears and anxieties out prior to surgery. The spiritual caregiver's aim is to enable the patient to go to surgery as relaxed as possible. A valuable goal.

In order to give the patient an opening to discuss feelings, the minister asks, "How are you?" The patient says, "I'm really not sure I'm ready for this. I didn't really get enough information from my doctor. I'm not clear about the operation and I'm kind of afraid."

The patient may appear to the spiritual care provider to need assurance and an opportunity to talk about feelings. They might go over the reasons for hospitalization and the events that led up to the condition. In the process of talking, the patient becomes more comfortable and relaxed. In this instance, a prayer for strength and God's presence during the surgery may be perfectly appropriate and may further aid the patient's ability to be as prepared for surgery as possible.

The minister in the previous scenario was not as concerned about the genesis of the anxiety as helping prepare the person for surgery. However, the patient's dis-ease may be more complex than simply not having enough information about the surgery. One option would have been to ask, "Can you tell me more about why you are afraid?"

In looking beyond the patient's presenting issues, deeper fears may be revealed, such as, "I am afraid I'll die without reconciling with my children." Looking for and allowing the expression of those fears not only helps allay the pre-surgery anxiety but focuses the support, affirmation, and prayer directly on the location of the person's struggle and pain. Although a pre-surgery visit is not the time to pressure people into sharing, it is vitally important to allow the patient the opportunity for that sharing.

About ten years ago I went into the hospital for hip replacement surgery. I was assured that it was a straightforward procedure and I would do well. Problem: After working in hospitals all my career, I had never been a patient in one; game changer! I had way more information than I needed for this experience. I also had great supportive clinicians around me, many of whom I had selected to care for me. As the day approached, I began to worry about my worry. It seemed there was more there than just overall anxiety about a new surgical experience. I had a nurse colleague who had been my partner in developing integrated medicine programs at the Cleveland Clinic. She asked me what was going on. That simple question and her caring enough to ask led to a discussion that changed my approach to the surgery. It didn't eliminate the anxiety but helped me manage it. We talked about why I was so worried and her observation that I had worked very hard to control everything I could about the procedure and why that was. We got to trust issues and why I wasn't trusting that others would care for me, including God. She then assured me that she would walk through the experience with me and see me in recovery. I felt a large burden lift. Putting words to what was bothering me and calling me to trust the Other in my life was on point and needed.

If we focus just on presenting issues, e.g., problem solving the crisis, or helping the person come to grips with the overt feelings, or moving the person past those feelings without considering the type of person they are and how they view the world and where the dis-ease in needs lie, we may miss the opportunity to hear what lies beneath.

Helen, whom I met after a seminar, shared her story with me. She talked about how her husband had died more than two years previously. She knew that she had become a burden both to the ministers in her church as well as to many of her friends. "They are tired of listening to me. I know I'm bothering them but I just can't seem to stop myself from talking. I know that I've been feeling this way for too long a period, but I just don't know how to stop."

After listening to her for a while, it became obvious to me that both ordained clergy and the laity in her congregation had made a spiritual care assessment. They had assessed a grief situation and had given her a chance to talk about her feelings during the period shortly after her husband's death. As the weeks went on, people became irritated that she was not moving past her feelings of grief. They would turn away when they saw her coming.

The question that had not been asked was how this situation affected how she was in the world and her needs. Nor had anyone asked her why she still grieved. The people trying to support her were well trained in the dynamics of grief, but how her basic understanding of herself and her needs had changed was left unattended.

When I asked for more information, she shared that in the space of a two-year period her mother died and her invalid father for whom she had cared died. She lost the home in which she had lived all her life. She could no longer afford to keep up a large house. She had to put her dog down, her constant companion for years. She now lived alone in a small apartment.

This is a complex and intense grief situation, probably more intense than the people responding to her realized. She had not only lost her loved ones, but she had also lost her purpose in life, her worth. She had been the caretaker for the sick people in her family for many years. She had not only lost her home and loved ones, but she had also lost her job. A job that everyone around her recognized as being a valuable one.

The steps to the process of sorting through Helen's presenting issues and assessing her type and dis-eased core need might be outlined as follows:

a. Listen and question.

b. Brainstorm a potential critical issue and need list.

    husband's death

    rejection from the congregation

    mother's death

    loss of home

    death of pet

    move to apartment

c. Distinguish

    a. Presenting issues

        rejection, grief, displacement

    b. Core issues, as in determining the person's type and core inner yearning and dis-eased need (or what impact on her life the presenting issues had): loss of worth and value, loss of home and self-identity. She lived her life as a Giver.

In all of the above situations, support people focused their helping around the presenting or critical issues rather than identifying and focusing on her type and the dis-ease in the need itself. Treating a dis-ease without considering its origins and its impact is *incomplete care*. In situations like this both the person in crisis and the support people may feel irritated and frustrated, and the problem may be extended or remain unresolved.

The chart and its categories below are how I distinguish presenting and core issues and how I isolate needs and types to inform my response.

Separating stimuli, reactions, potential responses, and feelings from types and needs has been helpful in distinguishing the type of person and their needs.

Stimuli	Responses	Reactions	Feelings	Type	Need
	Caregiver	Care receiver			

In ministry it is not unusual to gather a rather lengthy list of critical issues or stimuli and potential need areas or types. The list can happen very quickly. One of the most important reasons to choose a focus is that the response changes depending on which item of the chart is chosen.

For example, if you focus on feelings, which many people are trained to do, then the obvious goal is to help get the feeling out and share it. The thinking here is that sharing it will diminish its power and help the person feel better. If companionship or a listening ear is identified as the proper response, then a different path is selected. If relationships are talked about, then those issues may be focused on. The point here is that whatever you choose sets you on a path of care, and that path will differ from other topics followed.

The woman above is an example. People did a good job initially listening to her, bringing her meals, and supporting her. When their interventions didn't seem to help, they became frustrated. They didn't focus their care on her life commitment to be a Giver and the multiple ways that was now frustrated.

In our conversation, I first shared with her that I thought her grief was from several situations, not just one loss. This immediately got her attention. I asked her if she had been a part of a grief group. It had been suggested to her by her minister, but she had not followed through. I suggested she look at it again because there would certainly be people in the group who would have suffered multiple losses as she had. I asked if she had thought about how to replace the vocation of helping others. Again, she became interested and started thinking about how she might help others in her congregation. This was about a fifteen-minute conversation, but she walked away with what appeared to be more energy and more hope that there were new possibilities for her. Focusing on her type and needs while attending to her grief seemed to help.

Helen was lucky. She had a concerned minister and congregation surrounding her. I talked to the minister a couple of months later, and she told me Helen was coming to church regularly again and had agreed to be the coordinator of the home visitation group in the congregation. She also told the minister she was looking for a new apartment that would allow dogs in hopes she could get a new pet companion. New beginnings and new ways to give.

Type: Achiever
Need: Responsibility

Janet entered an acute care hospital with back pain, a suspected disc problem. She had recently been involved in an automobile accident. She had strong ties to her parents. Her father had died within the last two years and her mother had open heart surgery. Janet had a history of heart trouble.

The spiritual care provider in the situation felt Janet's relationship with her husband was shallow and characterized by a lack of communication. The husband was a quiet man and did not express his thoughts or feelings well. He had been drawing disability for several years for chronic back problems.

Janet presented herself cheerfully and calmly, saying she was in the hospital for a physical. All this information was gathered in a very short period of time, and the list of potential key issues was very long. Physically and emotionally, the presenting issues appeared to be her heart problems and her denial of them: "I'm in the hospital for a checkup." This situation could be defined as and treated as an unresolved grief situation over the death of her father and the potential loss of her mother.

The nursing staff saw her as a behavioral/emotional problem. They felt that Janet needed to stop accumulating the illnesses of those people around her. They felt she should be dealt with firmly and confrontationally around issues of diet, exercise, and manipulative behavior and planned to deal with her accordingly.

The spiritual care provider in the situation felt Janet was frightened. She thought it appropriate to help her ventilate some of those feelings so that she could look realistically at her physical situation and accept tests and treatment.

The staff who acted on their plan to be firm with her and confront her were met with firmness and stubbornness in return. Those who asked about her family problems and her husband's disability heard a long litany of ongoing problems but saw no apparent behavior change nor any decrease in her behavior.

The spiritual care provider, after initially helping her ventilate some of her feelings, began to look more closely for her yearning and dis-eased needs. What she heard was hidden anger and unspoken questions about why God was doing this to her. Janet was telling herself and everyone around her, "I have no responsibility; I can do nothing about all that is happening to me and I have a right to be angry. I'm the victim here."

Needs Assessment Chart for Janet
Brainstorm List of Issues (Assessed by the Minister)

Father's death

Mother's illness

Husband's illness

Anger

Fear

Accumulating illnesses

Blames others

Help her share feelings

Cheerful exterior

Denial of reality

Help her become realistic about her illness

The list above can be broken out into the following categories:

Stimuli	Responses	Reactions	Feelings	Type	Need
Father's death Mother's illness Her illness Husband's illness	Share feelings Get her realistic	Her illnesses Blame Initially cheerful	Fear Anger	Achiever (I'm the victim) Others are doing this to me	Reconciliation and responsibility

The overall assessment we can make of Janet from the chart is that she was blocked by anger and, as a result, was unwilling to accept responsibility for her role in the situation. The minister assessed that she was an Achiever, someone who blamed others first. She had difficulty in accepting responsibility for her actions. She didn't undervalue herself; she blamed others and undervalued them. The response for this dis-eased need and for this type is in helping her learn how to take responsibility for her actions in relationships. In this case, being right and avoiding blame took precedent over relationships.

This is a different assessment than unresolved grief or labeling her a manipulative hypochondriac or treating her solely as a heart patient. All the presenting issues mentioned are important and certainly need to be dealt with but should be attended to while understanding the life context and her inner yearning.

Type: Giver
Need: Worth

Britany, a woman in her early twenties, had a history of hospitalizations in a mental health unit of a community hospital. She had experienced much rejection from her family, particularly from her father. She had been abused physically by her father and had often been depressed and withdrawn. She was given to periods of anger, striking out at those around her, and voicing that no one cared.

Using the categories in the previous diagram helps clarify where to focus the response.

Needs Assessment Chart for Britany
Brainstorm List

I'm not worth much

Companionship

Outgoing

Striking out

Anger

Father's beatings

Family rejection

Mental health hospital

Behavior modification

Listening

The invitation is to put into a brainstorm list whatever sounds important that could call for a spiritual care response.

With a list like the above, where do you start? What is most important? How do you decide. Clarifying which category each should go in should help to identify the core issues of type and need.

The chart below helps.

Stimuli	Responses	Reactions	Feelings	Type	Need
Beatings, rejection	Companionship, love	Anger, striking out	Anger, loneliness		I'm not worth much
Lack of safety	Listening ear	Depression and withdrawal			

Rejection and abuse are not dis-eased needs; they are stimuli that can cause the dis-ease. They do not describe the impact on the person and the way he or she chooses to live because of it. Anger is a feeling that can help us understand the basic approach of that person to their situation; but it is not a dis-eased *need* or her *type*. Companionship or listening or "being with" are potential *responses* of the minister to the person's situation. There are *reactions* that come from the person, such as withdrawal or acting out, but those situations are reactions to something that has been depleted or disrupted in their lives. They are not dis-eased needs stemming from her type.

Dis-eased need? Britany gave us a pretty good clue. All of the sad events in her story left her with the belief that "I'm not worth much."

Very different care plans emerge depending on the chosen focus. If we choose to help this woman deal with her anger, we take one direction. If we decide to use behavior modification to keep her from striking out at others, we use a different focus for a treatment plan. If we decide that the focus should be on loving her and valuing her as an important person, we get another focus.

The purpose of the chart is to focus on her type and core needs and help the minister choose where to respond. If the father's beatings are put in the stimulus category and feelings are listed and reactions are logged, then the choices for needs are narrowed. In

Britany's case one "needs" item on the potential list comes the closest. "I'm not worth much."

It appeared initially that she was a Giver, and her doubt of her worth was the dis-ease in her perception of her value.

Outward anger and aggression and blaming others are often signs of an Achiever or one who puts their needs before others. Britany had multiple problems, and it appeared that she struck out to save herself from complete despair. There was very little giving in her story, probably because of the pain. Focusing on her need for worth would let us know quickly where the primary need lay and give us hints at her core type.

The key would be looking for whether she was truly blaming others (Achiever) or blaming herself. ("There is something wrong with me that is causing my problems": Giver). We can choose to respond to any part of her story, but keeping one eye on her type and need brings depth to the care.

What happened with these women? The chaplain who was working with Britany shared his thoughts with the rest of the care team. The team then included positive image reinforcement as part of the care plan. They began to see lessening of the aggression she had shown to caregivers, and the team began to like her more and that improved the relationship. The team included self-worth activities in her post hospital plan, and hope grew for Britany's improvement.

Janet was a tougher case. She had built her life around being the victim while putting forward a positive face. She deflected any attempts to give her feedback about her behavior. People involved with her presented treatment options that focused on what would be good for her. They talked about goals she had for her life and how she might achieve them. This diminished her resistance to what had been suggested to her. This was a beginning with a tough road ahead.

Types and Needs

Type: Searcher
Need: Commitment

John, a middle-aged architect, walked into a minister's office in a local parish one day and began to talk to the minister about some dissatisfactions he had been feeling during the last few months. As the minister asked him to tell more it became apparent that the man seemed comfortable with his chosen profession. He was a successful architect making a considerable amount of money. He felt that his relationships with his wife and family were going well. It was a strong family, committed to one another, and they were weathering the challenges of raising adolescent children. He was consistent in his church involvement. He had listened to the sermons and the challenges to bring his faith into the workplace.

John had become increasingly frustrated with the high pressure of continuing to make money. He had initiated conversations with his partner about projects that would more directly benefit people. He had a long-standing interest in housing for disabled people and the elderly and wanted to develop creative designs that would make their living situations easier. His partner was not interested in the idea and did not want to consider the possibilities because the financial benefits were not clear.

John's concerns had grown to the point where he felt stuck and did not know how to proceed. His family had grown comfortable with the lifestyle his successful business had provided. He began to think that he needed to change jobs. He considered going to seminary.

The minister thought that the "stimuli" for John's predicament was a growing dissatisfaction with his job, triggered by challenges from his involvement in the church and middle-age revaluation. John had not been able to adjust in his workplace. The minister's considered response was to help John share his feelings, to journey with him in his story, and to help him deal with the mid-life evaluation.

The minister sensed that John's dis-eased need was in his commitment to meaning and purpose in life. It seemed that the meaning he had lodged in being successful and a good architect no longer held value for him. He felt lost. John's type at this point in his life was that of a Searcher. He had some ideas of paths he might take, a glimpse of a dream, but he needed encouragement, direction, and the courage required to pay the price of a new path.

John eventually talked to his wife and then his children about a plan to start his own company focusing on creating buildings for those with special needs. The conversations were difficult, as the reality of less salary and the need for startup money impacted them. His wife had been an interior designer prior to focusing her work on the home and the kids. She was comfortable in their lifestyle and with their friends and didn't initially want to risk changing. It appeared that they might have to sell the house they lived in and downsize to get some startup money. The kids, twelve and fifteen years old, reacted. It helped that they could stay in their school, but they did not want to leave their neighborhood.

After months of conversation and counsel from their minister, John's wife began to feel some excitement about having a designer role in this new company. Her excitement and the conversations with the kids freed John to make concrete plans to move ahead with this life change.

It was June when they decided to leap and begin their new adventure. They sold their house very quickly, gave up their country club membership, and moved into a more modest area. The company began to be successful much more quickly than anticipated, helped primarily by local and federal seed money for these kinds of projects. Their first project was a new kind of building for adults with limited mobility; funded by their city and the state.

Summary

There are three needs and three types. Any or all our needs can be dis-eased in crisis. Our type determines our primary need, which is our default position in crisis.

Primary needs and types call for primary attention and specific responses. Distinguishing between them helps us gather the appropriate responses. One of the ways that has helped me distinguish between the types and needs is to listen to how people talk about themselves.

a. Achievers very often say, "I'm angry; it's your fault; I won't change;" and lay the responsibility for the problems they are experiencing outside of themselves.

b. Givers may often say something like, "I'm a mess; it is my fault; I can't change." These people see themselves as the unwilling creators of the problems that they are experiencing.

c. Searchers may say, "I'm lost; I don't know what to change" and have trouble defining the problem and knowing what to do, or they fear the definition will limit them.

Diacritics need to choose when they are faced with a multiple list of issues in people's lives. The types and needs category can be used to sort out the difference between needs and feelings, between needs and stimuli that trigger dis-ease, and between needs and the reactions and responses that are the results of the dis-ease.

Spiritual care providers tend to generalize the differences between needs, thinking that the three areas come from one source, i.e., a need for love or worth. They often feel the areas are so general that they don't want to choose. People and the need areas that get dis-eased, however, are very different.

Types and Needs Areas and Basic Views

Assessing people's type and needs and discovering where there is unmet yearning or dis-ease in their need areas is an exercise for the purpose of evaluation and goal setting in our spiritual care relationships. The gathering of information, sensing and understanding what is truly being said, looking for the meaning behind the words has a great measure of art in it. A structured look at needs works with intuition to direct the response.

What follows is a more in-depth look at the three types and need areas and case examples that demonstrate their differences.

Section 1: Spiritual Care Assessment

Achievers and Responsibility

Achievers often see others as the main source of their difficulties. Vulnerability for these people means having blame laid at their doorstep. They feel they are right and see no reason to change. The world or others in relationship to them need to change before their relations can be improved. It is often men who are acculturated in our society to turn blame outside of themselves and to place responsibility on others and the world for their situations. They often attack instead of remaining open to receive. They need to look at their own responsibility before they can act on the crisis that confronts them.

A while back I got into a conversation at an airport with Larry, whom I had met at a professional meeting. He and I began to talk about the state of men's and women's relationships. Larry mentioned that he was recently divorced. The announcement that his wife wanted a divorce, according to him, came out of the blue at a dinner on their wedding anniversary. He had been divorced almost a year and still had no idea why she had divorced him. When I asked Larry what his wife gave as her reasons, he said she felt depressed in the relationship and felt she had given him many significant hints about the difficulties in their marriage, but he had not listened. She felt her only alternative was to ask for a divorce.

Larry listed the ways in which he had supported his wife. He had paid and supported her way through college; he had begun to help with some of the housework to free her for her job and schooling. He did not understand why his wife felt powerless in the relationship. He saw her as a strong person. Now, a year after the divorce, he was still confused and angry and refused to accept responsibility for his part. Larry blamed her irresponsibility and lack of commitment to their fifteen-year relationship.

When I asked him if he could remember any of the times that his wife had talked about troubles in their relationship, he remembered two. When I asked him if she had ever suggested counseling, he admitted she had raised the subject but that he had not seen the need for it and told her he was not willing to do it at that time. It became clear that Larry was not ready to bring any resolution to his past marriage or to build new relationships until he dealt with these issues.

A second example of someone who as an Achiever had dis-ease in her ability to accept responsibility in relationships was Sarah, a conservative protestant minister who was a part of a clinical pastoral education group. She had been abused as a child and had found some resolution and healing through her faith and through her relationship with the church. In her training and in her floor work, Sarah was seen by many people as assertive and sometimes aggressive; she was clearly the leader in her peer group. She could be volatile and did not hesitate to make her needs or wants known. She often pointed out the problems of her peers in direct fashion. In the early stages of her training program, she was nicknamed the Assistant Educator even though she was on the same level as the others. Sarah saw herself as a kind, nurturing minister and peer. She emphasized love and affirmation in her preaching and in her direct ministry with patients, or so she thought. There were many times when the tragedy of her childhood and her struggles with her vocation and spiritual care made those around her think of her as a Giver and self-worth as her primary dis-eased need. She asked for nurture, was angry with me whenever I challenged her, and did not agree at all with my assessment of her that she could be an aggressive, firm, and somewhat distant minister and peer. When I interviewed her patients, they commented that they respected her, that she represented "tough love." They experienced her as somewhat distant, not forthcoming with personal history, and not vulnerable. This feedback did not match at all with Sarah's understanding of herself; even when faced with direct feedback, she had great difficulty accepting it because it did not correspond with her own concepts of herself.

This situation is not at all unusual, particularly with people who are very religious or who have strong family or cultural values and norms against anger or against laying blame on other people. With Sarah, it was sinful to blame others or to act out of anger. Her initial presentation of herself made her appear to be a person who blamed herself. She would often talk about how her problem was self-blame. Peers, some of her patients ,and educators often felt blamed by her.

The task with Sarah and others like her who are Achievers and have dis-ease in their ability to take responsibility in relationships is to look honestly at their relationships and to accept feedback from those who come to know them.

Givers and Worth

The Giver, as noted, is the one who says most often, "It's my fault and I can't change." These are people who feel powerless in the face of situations that surround them. Self-worth is their struggle. When a crisis occurs, they blame themselves. Crises do not mobilize them; they turn the responsibility inward and often get down and feel powerless.

Givers need to experience themselves as valuable and as people with power before they can begin to react to situations differently and create new resources with which to cope.

Gloria, a forty-two-year-old woman, walked into her parish pastor's office in a panic. She told the minister that while she was driving her car the previous day, she almost opened the door and jumped out as the car was moving. Gloria had four children ranging in age from ten to nineteen. She had recently lost a considerable amount of weight. She had started a new job, her first job outside the home. She was feeling good about her job and her boss was supportive. Gloria was proud of her new independence and felt comfortable in her job. However, she was not getting support at home. There was little communication between Gloria and her husband, and she felt she was not getting the respect and support for her new growth from him and from her older children. Her husband had recently questioned her ability to run the family finances and had taken that job away from her. The only money now available to Gloria was the money she was making from her own job. This was sufficient to meet her needs but she was reeling under the accusation and lack of trust. These tensions had grown so great that she had been staying with a friend occasionally rather than going home. She couldn't face the negative comments and lack of support.

Gloria had been a consistent churchgoer in this parish but left because things were not going well for her and she felt the church had not helped. Her potential needs list is extensive. Her chart follows.

Needs Assessment Chart

Brainstorm List

Anger at God

Anger at spouse

No support

New job

Weight loss

Family finances taken away

Jumping from the car

Desire for respect

Forty-two years old

Staying away from home

Leaving church

Stimuli	Response	Reaction	Feelings	Type	Need
No support New job God and church Family finances Forty-two years old	Talk about conflict in her marriage	Wants respect Panic Staying away from home Leaving church Weight loss	Anger at spouse	Giver	Self-worth

Gloria wanted a sense of self-achievement and seemed to be searching for a life purpose outside of her family responsibilities. The minister considered the conflict in her relationship with her husband. She appeared to be blocked by her anger and confused about how to resolve it or how to use her anger creatively. She was also searching for a new self-concept. This seemed blocked by uncertainty of her value, particularly when challenged by her family. She also appeared to be struggling for new meaning and new direction. That struggle seemed distinct from her interior self-acceptance and guilt around putting her needs before others.

It is important to decide which is the primary need. Offering support and affirmation for Gloria's new self-concept as a primary plan requires different responses from the spiritual care provider than supporting her in the conflict between herself and family members or supporting her as she grows into her new job.

Some questions to consider in selecting the primary dis-eased needs are: Had Gloria decided to leave her family and pursue her own goals but was holding back because of her understanding of herself, her church commitments, and her upbringing?

Did she need permission and support to act? If that is the case, then it would lead us toward a Giver's worth needs. Did she feel blocked from achieving her goals because she was angry and in conflict with her husband? If so, the dis-ease would come from being an Achiever.

Searching for meaning and purpose, although an important factor, did not seem to be the primary need that was disrupted. Gloria had generated enough energy to redefine herself and her role in life. The risks and growth that she was experiencing brought her a significant sense of accomplishment and helped her feel good about herself. As the family members around her were experiencing her in a new way and were not supportive, she began to feel panicky.

The panic came from beginning to face the price that living in a new way was going to exact from her, particularly in her relationship with her husband and children.

Gloria had not yet built a new community for herself in which her new growth, maturity, and freedom would get the support it needed to be nourished and to continue to grow. This was a woman with significant resources, but her new emerging sense of worth needed to be fostered.

Jack was a man in his early twenties placed in a mental hospital by his wife. He was the picture of macho. He was a weight lifter and wore T-shirts with cigarettes rolled in the sleeves. The priest who was the chaplain for his floor area was small and aesthetic looking. Jack would tell the chaplain how he and his buddies would close bars and take on all comers. Jack told stories about how he made sure that all the women in his life were "in their place." On occasion, he would ask the priest if he was ever lonely or afraid.

The priest, in conversations with me, would talk about how Jack threatened and angered him. The priest initially responded to Jack's taunts with defensiveness and anger.

Needs Assessment Chart for Jack

Brainstorm List of Critical Issues and Needs

Macho

Apprehensive

Drinking

Close ties to buddies

Dominant approach to women

Challenges to weakness

Weight lifting

Boasting

Self-image

Committed to state hospital

The list above can be broken out into the following categories:

Section 1: Spiritual Care Assessment

Stimuli	Response	Reaction	Feelings	Type	Need
Commit-ted to the state hospital		Drinking			
		Stories of macho bud-dies, boasting, dominant with women, weight lift-ing, fights and challenges			

As the priest stopped fighting and became sensitive to Jack's fear, Jack talked of not belonging, of not having a place where he could feel valued with his feelings. His self-image and worth had been shattered because of forced hospitalization. He felt he had no community in which to piece it together again. Jack's outward behavior reflected his anger and spite. When the minister in the situation stopped fighting with the externals, Jack very quickly got into the pain and the fear and the inadequacy that he felt. He had been deeply hurt by having to enter a mental hospital against his will. He may have once felt that everyone else was at fault but finally realized that he truly had very few resources with which to live in this world and feel capable.

Jack was ready for a change when the minister walked into his life. After the minister stopped reacting out of his own issues and started responding to Jack's, Jack was able to engage.

Jack was tough to assess because he did not have the outward persona of a giver or someone who struggled with worth. He had taken on the persona of someone who got things done, who achieved. This persona covered his worth issues and the blame he assigned to himself.

Searchers and Commitment

People with dis-ease in the commitment required for a meaning and purpose need very often talk about feeling lost and not knowing how to change or how to go about getting their life back on track. They can be afraid that choosing can limit opportunity.

They have enough energy; they just need to know where or how to direct it. They are distinct from the self-worth person in that they don't blame themselves for their condition, they just are confused and uncertain about who to blame or how to move.

We all need to be committed to something outside of ourselves that can fulfill us. When our ability to create or find fulfilling opportunities is blocked, we get frustrated, restless, and uncertain. Whereas giving self-worth people suggestions may burden them, giving suggestions to meaning and direction people can often be energizing and can get them to commit to a path.

We all have all three types and needs as a part of us. While we have a dominant type, multiple trauma or difficult events can throw our other types and needs out of balance. Such is the case with Helen, who was in grief and whose parish had tired of her grieving. This woman had lost her job and her purpose for being. She was seen as someone who was very skilled in caring for others. Helen had cared for all her immediate family members. She was an outgoing, well-liked person, but her need to keep talking about the people that she had lost began to wear on her friends. Helen needed a new direction, new meaning in which to place her energy. As she and I talked about her situation, she noticeably brightened when I suggested that her next conversation with her pastor could be a conversation in which she would ask him if he knew of any situations in the parish where Helen might use the caretaking skills that she had developed over the years.

Helen's reaction would be very different from a self-worth person's whose response would probably be to sigh and begin to think of several reasons why that conversation should not take place.

Another example is Jane, who was struggling with depressed feelings. She was a fifty-year-old woman who had two children and a husband. Her daughter was twenty-five and had recently moved to a southern state to continue her career. Her son was twenty-two, just finishing college, and had decided to move to the West Coast and take a job with a firm in California. It was clear that this woman's problems began about the time her children moved away from home. Her husband was generally supportive of her and had stuck by her through her hospitalization.

In conversations with Jane, she was initially hesitant to talk about new possibilities for her future. When asked about her children and the meaning she placed in her care of them, a picture emerged of a woman who had totally invested herself in caring for children who were now grown and were moving away. Jane had not been educated beyond high school. She had done none of the money managing in her family and had no idea what resources she had for new directions. Her children were beginning to get angry with her because she would often call them and ask them to come home.

The above approach sounds simplistic, but it is appropriate for people who are confused and stuck. When a person who is a Searcher struggles with commitment and has meaning and purpose issues challenging them, offering new ideas and offering support in trying on new behavior is helpful to them. Searchers often get stuck at the point of paying the price for the new behavior, as the architect did in a previous example.

Searchers can at times appear to be Givers; however, they are not people who are blaming themselves or whose self-deprecation keeps them from moving. They are genuinely lost, struggling with commitment and uncertain as to how to proceed.

Lawrence LeShan in his writings talks about how important this need area is in the treatment of seriously ill people, particularly cancer patients. One of his main suggestions for renewing health and raising the resources of people with whom he works is that they commit themselves to something outside of themselves. When such commitment is absent, the person is more susceptible to physical challenges, especially when the patient's meaning is blocked by trauma or outside forces that seem more powerful than their ability to cope.[3]

---

3. LeShan, *Mechanic and the Gardener*, 34.

Summary

Like any professional caregiver, the diacritic or spiritual care assessor needs to decide what type of person they are dealing with and what need area is dis-eased or is being yearned for. The plan for care then flows out of that assessment.

One of the major ways to identify the type and the primary dis-eased need is to note how people respond to some of our reactions to them. The Achiever will turn it outward and blame others; the Giver will turn confrontation inward and blame themselves; the Searcher does not commit to blaming anyone and may well be energized by it if it points a new path forward.

Supporting or showing care may move the Giver into action, may confirm the Achiever's position that they are not responsible, and may leave the Searcher stuck in the same place. Insight may interest the Searcher, overwhelm the Giver, and leave the Achiever unaffected.

It is important that we distinguish and focus our care on the type and primary need that is dis-eased. The responses that help people and the resources people bring to bear on the crises facing them are very different and impact them differently.

We turn our attention to the next task of the diacritic or spiritual care assessor, and that is to describe the need of the person theologically or spiritually.

6

The Language of Ritual and Spiritual Practice

THE SPIRITUAL ASSESSOR NEEDS to place the needs in the language of spirituality or theology. I've seen several attempts at this; the most common is trying to find spiritual needs that can be distinguished from other disciplines. Sometimes that's successful, e.g., a need for reverence of the Holy Other; sometimes not, e.g., hope, a more generic word that can be used by many disciplines. One of the problems is that there is very little consistency from list to list.

My suggestion is that we look to our rituals or high holidays or holy stories to find the theological and spiritual language for spiritual care assessment and for the introduction to spiritual care response.

I think it's been difficult to look to ritual for spiritual care assessment for two reasons. The first is that rituals have become so much a part of our practice that their efficacy is often placed in the observance rather than in the relationship truths that are held within them.

The second is that rituals are where, in religious and spiritual practice, rigidity and legalism are often held, whether that's in Hebrew scripture with its clarity on how to live or in early Christianity and Islam and the dictums for daily living.

54

The Language of Ritual and Spiritual Practice

In the early part of the twentieth century, Christian ministers normally expected people to fit into the theological constructs around them. With the advent of the industrial revolution and the professionalism of health care chaplaincy, social work, and psychology, fitting theology to a person's situation or needs became important.

The rebellion we see historically in response to religious rigidity and in some religious practice may have been a necessary step, because it broke the pattern of rigid ways of expecting people to conform their lives to theological constructs rather than having the theology or spirituality dialogue with people about the meaning of their lives. It becomes even more important in these days when more people are claiming to be spiritual rather than religious.

There is rich wisdom and language in our rituals that should not be ignored. The reason is that there are *relationship truths* in our rituals that can guide us. In addition, there are more similarities than differences in the wisdom of our religious and spiritual traditions across culture and beliefs.

I believe that there are many systems that can be used in describing people's spiritual or theological dis-ease. I believe, however, that what is important is not so much the system used for the language but the commitment to a process that assesses people and their situations theologically or spiritually. Any system is viable for the spiritual caregiver as well as for the people for whom we care when it is in tune with people's dynamics and the relationship issues that they face.

This is not a process shrouded in mystery. The next natural step for the diacritic following type and needs identification is to brainstorm the holy writings, rituals, theological images and stories, and spiritual concepts within their traditions or the rituals of the person for whom they care.

Regis Duffy in his book *Real Presence* discusses his concern about Christian sacraments becoming so ritualized that they no longer impact people. He calls us back to understand that what we have ritualized must have real meaning and validity for our lives:

"Worship not only symbolizes God's presence but our response to it. Just as this worship must bear the marks of our current and past history, so too must it symbolize our new commitments to God's work wrung out of our conflicts."[1]

For the spiritual care person, the relationship truths found in our rituals, stories, ordinances, and wisdom literature that have been passed on from generation to generation can be living guidelines for the movements of relationships and can offer spiritual care assessment and response direction.

Angeles Arrien, a noted anthropologist and writer was my teacher and a friend. Her work in *The Four-Fold Way* and other books looks across cultures and traditions of indigenous peoples and finds common movements and processes for the maturation of the human spirit.

The conclusion for me is that the rituals handed down through centuries would not have been handed down if they did not have personal and relationship truths in them.

The holy stories, liturgies and rituals, and concepts come to us over the centuries, out of the stuff of relationships and the journeys of people. They have been molded out of the important questions and issues of life. Rituals and liturgies may have been used so long that they have become ritualized. They may be so institutionalized that the real-life truths tucked in them have been forgotten. Also forgotten may be the signposts and paths that can help frame the next steps for the person taking the journey as well as for the spiritual caregiver.

Arrien in *The Four-Fold Way* has the medicine man or shaman ask the one coming for care the following: "When in your life did you stop singing? When in your life did you stop dancing? When in your life did you stop being enchanted by stories, particularly your own story?"[2]

In most cultures and religions there are community welcoming ceremonies, coming of age stories, and redemption stories. In these rituals are the steps that lead from dis-ease to healing.

1. Duffy, *Real Presence*, 78.
2. Arrien, *Four-Fold Way*, 54.

Donald Capps in his book *Pastoral Care: A Thematic Approach* has taken Erik Erikson's development stages to do his needs assessment and then used Pruyser's theological concepts to assess people theologically.[3]

In other places I've seen the seven deadly sins used to spiritually assess where people are in their journeys and to name those dynamics spiritually.

Stories can help us understand our own stories and journeys. The rich stories in holy writings are the stories of life and of struggle.

The twelve-step process of Alcoholics Anonymous knows this well. They have defined the steps that will bring repair and renewal.

In most rituals across cultures there are clear steps to be taken to either gain or return to balance and wholeness. I have chosen three areas to take a closer look at.

a. Responsibility/reconciliation: Taking personal responsibility in relationships

b. Community: Finding healing partnerships in a group

c. Vocation: A call to something beyond ourselves

The three can be found in most religions and spiritual paths across cultures, often in different forms but with surprisingly similar processes.

A Jewish rabbi and I had a conversation about spiritual assessment. He had a great deal of difficulty relating to anything that had a sense of Christian sacraments or ordinances until we looked at the relationship truths inherent in them. His mind immediately went to the stories in Hebrew scriptures. He could not relate to Eucharist and communion; he could, however, understand the high holy days and the stories in scripture as holding relationship truths with processes that move people to wholeness. Yom Kippur with its emphasis on making amends and asking for forgiveness echoes what we see in other practices of religions and forms of spirituality,

3. Capps, *Pastoral Care*, 114.

where repair is needed in relationships. The Adam and Eve story was a story of responsibility and reconciliation. The steps that Adam and Eve took to move from being apart to being reconciled again were precisely the relationship movements that are found in Christian communion and Eucharist.

I was in my office in the hospital one day during Yom Kippur and heard a knock on my door. My boss, a devout Jew, was dropping in as he periodically did. He shocked me that day by saying he was coming to ask my forgiveness for the acts he had done or had not done that may have offended me over the last year. I quickly reassured him that he had been great with us and began to tell him how much I appreciated him. He would have none of the quick forgiveness I was offering. He knew that we had not yet talked about how he had fallen short in our relationship. What followed was a heartfelt conversation of what might have been and some events that could have been avoided. It allowed me to follow with where I had missed the mark and where I needed forgiveness. Forgiveness was asked for and given that day and plans were made on how to move forward.

A Hindu student I've been working with in a doctoral program shared with me the similarities between some of the Christian rituals she was seeing in the seminary where she was studying with some of the movements of Hinduism. She said that karma is like the concept of forgiveness, for when harm is done the person is to know what they have done wrong and if they act in forgiveness, they will find peace. The sacred thread ceremony, an initiation rite, marks the official acceptance of a boy into his *varna* and he becomes twice born into community. The last rite she shared was the call to priesthood where one is committed to a greater purpose.

The stages in the rituals are normally sequential. A person can't start with absolution or new beginnings before they have confessed they've fallen short or before they make amends. It makes relationship sense. It is important to identify those actions before the person has some understanding of the behavior that needs to be changed. Alcoholics Anonymous knows this just as Yom Kippur knows this as the shaman knows it as Islam knows it.

Like any other process that people go through, some stages are more difficult than others. Some people get stuck in the process; others refuse to move. The old familiar patterns may be too comfortable, the new behaviors called for may extract too great a price. Whatever the case, when a person gets stuck and is not able to cope or to bring some resolution to their struggle, then illness and unhealthy behavior may result. When people have unresolved conflict with a parent, family member, or friend over the years, that dis-ease eats away at them and at their body.

There are places in each of these ritual areas where the spiritual caregiver may get stuck. These are places where they limit themselves in being able to respond and move to new understanding. In reconciliation that place seems to be around judgment or acknowledgment. In the Christian church's more recent history, spiritual caregivers were much into forgiveness and absolving people. Some are still living in an age of hesitancy about bringing judgment, calling people to repentance, or calling them to acknowledge their part in the problem.

Bringing judgment when someone is stuck at acknowledging their part of the problem is precisely what is needed at the beginning of the reconciliation process. Making this assessment does not define how that judgment will be brought into the relationship when the person is slow to acknowledgment. It assesses, however, that it is necessary. There is a difference between being judgmental with someone (condemning them) and calling them to acknowledge their shortfalls and calling them to repentance.

Responsibility and Reconciliation

It seems to me that the movements within this ritual area are the struggles of broken relationships, with people in conflict and apart from others, the Holy, and themselves. This area holds a call to responsibility and recognition of one's own role in the conflict and separation.

Duffy talks about the condemnation passages of the New Testament in Christian Scriptures in his book around the ritual of Eucharist. He says those who eat without bonding or loving others or committing to reconcile broken relationships risk eating to their own condemnation. He ties Christian Scripture, liturgy, and Eucharist together with real people's struggles. One truth emerging here is that without calling oneself to responsibility and accepting one's responsibility in a broken relationship, there cannot be a move to absolution and reconciliation within the relationship.[4]

The ritual area of responsibility and reconciliation is intended to mend relationships and to bring truth and life through loving ourselves and others. The stages of this ritual area can be found in our liturgies, spiritual and religious gatherings, our catechisms, our memorial meals, our holy days, wherever there are rites of confession, repair, and renewal. The stages in this area, as in the other areas, then become a road map for moving from separateness and conflict to reconciliation, absolution, and forgiveness and beginning anew.

Stages of Reconciliation/Responsibility

The steps in reconciliation follow:

a. Acknowledgment or judgment. This is that moment when we are willing to say, "This is my problem; I have fallen short in this relationship." It is moving away from the stance that the other person is the one to blame.

b. Confession or naming the sin or shortcoming. This is being sorry or contrite while naming those acts that have offended.

b. Repentance is turning away from the behavior that we have confessed. It is one thing to name our behavior and feel sorry for it. It is quite another to turn away from it and toward a new life. Old patterns, even when painful and destructive,

---

4. Duffy, *Real Presence*, 148–49.

can hold an attraction and familiarity for us that can make turning away difficult.

d. Making amends, or penance in some traditions, is that step that calls us to try on the new behavior that is different from what we have confessed and from which we have turned. In a relationship where a lot of harm has been done, quick confessions or judgments sometimes have been a part of previous unsuccessful resolutions. Making amends is a demonstration of our genuineness and a demonstration that we know what needs to be changed and are willing to take the risks inherent in changing those specific parts of our behavior.

e. Absolution is that final sense of forgiving ourselves, of living out of being a forgiven person. It is different than continuing to seek and being afraid and uncertain of our freedom to be our whole self. In relationship terms it is the actual absolving of people in relationship with one another. It is making the conflict history slate clean, starting anew. It is the "I now believe that you are different" statement that is needed in a relationship if it is to move on.

In my experience with reconciliation, the point where people most often get stuck is at the beginning of the process. They need to acknowledge their part in the problem. Judging oneself as the wrongdoer or the sinner in the situation seems to be one of the most difficult things to do for an Achiever. Once a person can acknowledge their part, put words to what is needed, the turning away from the behavior seems to be easier. Changing the behavior, doing the amends, and believing in forgiveness are more difficult because of the price they exact.

The difficulty with absolution is believing in personal forgiveness and acting on it. People can live with their hostilities and anger so long that they are familiar partners and are not easy to give up.

For Britany, the young woman in the mental health ward of a hospital from chapter 5, a brainstorm list might include thoughts about reconciliation and self-worth. She seems to need to see her value. She needs to know that she is special in God's sight: "Consider the lilies of the field." The middle-aged architect may recall the prophets or disciples or holy teachers being called from their professions or stations in life into new ways of living.

Janet, who seemed to be accumulating illnesses from her mother and husband and was not dealing very realistically with her illnesses, might remind the diacritic of Ps 23. She was an "up Christian" who had tried to live on the positive side of things. She tried to turn the bad times to good times, usually at the expense of her feelings. She may need to learn how to walk through the valley of the shadow of death rather than trying to stay out of it.

The caregiver in the situation began to talk with her and realized that Janet felt others were to blame. She had questions about why things happened to her. She felt she had no responsibility for her actions and the way that she was living her life. Until she could acknowledge that she had a role and responsibility in what was happening to her, she was not going to be able to move to new life and a new sense of forgiveness and freedom.

There is no absolution or forgiveness without judgment of one's actions in any tradition or culture. There were different ways of calling Janet to account. One way was used by the floor staff, who had decided that she was manipulative and needed some clear messages about her behavior. They met considerable resistance in their approach. The major reason, with implications for spiritual care assessment and spiritual care response, is that the resistance came because the nursing staff were holding themselves apart from Janet. They were not in relationship with her while calling her to account. They were not in the process with her. They were standing outside the process and being judgmental.

In Christian Scriptures, Jesus' relationship with the woman at the well in the book of John (4:5–30) was a call for her to claim responsibility for her life, to move beyond it and receive new life. The context of the story was set within the initial interaction when Jesus, a Jew, talked with and accepted a drink from a Samaritan woman. He took unusual steps to involve himself with her. He showed he was willing to risk being in relationship. She was prepared then to accept his words and call to judgment and to be involved with him.

There are numerous examples of how prophets, holy ones, and holy leaders call people to be different, to accept their lot, and to move beyond. That is the sense of the reconciliation process. To move beyond being apart from others means being able to acknowledge our part in keeping ourselves estranged.

Community: Finding Our Worth

The next ritual area I call community. The invitation is to find our worth while living in a new way in a new community. We can find these processes in Christianity in baptism and confirmation, in Judaism in bar and bat mitzvah, and with indigenous peoples in ceremonies with vision questing, wherever there are initiations or belonging and entering ceremonies. Ingredients of that sense of community have consistent parts and patterns to it. Belonging, entering, finding a place to grow and be refreshed, committing to change and new life are themes of the area of community.

Robert Kegan says, "In a community worthy of its name there are symbols and celebrations, retreat even gesture by which I am knowing the process of my development, by which I am helped to recognize myself . . . communities . . . have always found ways to recognize a person's growth and change."[5]

It is in community where people can find their identity and worth, where they can risk changing with the certainty that they belong. Community then is the theological or spiritual name and word for finding our self-worth. It is the theological or spiritual response to our need to be valued.

The people of Israel have this theme throughout the scriptures in that they are constantly being called back into being the people of God when they stray. It is in community where they have identity and their worth in being people of the Holy One. The message throughout these rituals is that the Holy One's people

5. Kegan et al., *Toward Moral and Religious Maturity*, 426.

are chosen and set apart. Their worth is measured by whose they are, rather than by what they do or what they can accomplish on their own.

Stages of Community

a. Recognition of being alone

b. Need for community

c. Confession

d. Decision for new life

In the United States today there seems to be a significant part of some religious groups that feed on people's pain and desire for belonging and living in community. People can contribute to religious organizations through television, radio, or online and feel like they are a part of something. It is the implicit and sometimes explicit expectation that they will get something in return that will give them a sense of belonging.

At the same time there is a huge shift from membership in religious organizations, to being spiritual rather than religious.

I spent almost twenty years living in and around San Francisco. Membership in churches was very low. However, I have never lived in a place where there was more talk and commitment concerning things spiritual. The need to belong, to find meaning was as strong as in other parts of the country where church membership was high.

There are many communities that emphasize welcoming people into community and stepping apart from what is happening around them. The cleansing and turning away from the old and embracing the new can be offered in rigid and demanding ways that are not really a decision for a new life within our world. For many people in "mainstream religious communities" in the US, it is commonplace to be a part of the community, to go through the rites and symbols on our individual Sabbaths, and to continue our patterns of living unaffected by the way we are called from the community.

The same is true in spiritual care situations where people struggle for their own sense of worth. It is an easy thing to claim our need for community, to recognize we are alone, and to recognize what needs to be changed. I have found that people most often get stuck in their decision for a new life, in the commitment to living in a different way. It is difficult because the old way is often a long-time companion, even if it is not healthy and has brought unhealthy results. It is familiar territory, and changes are unfamiliar territory.

Gloria, the woman who had considered jumping out of a moving car, faced some clear decisions about how she wanted to live her life and what was called forth from her. She had made some startling moves to find new ways to understand herself. She had gotten some support, a new job, had felt good about herself, and was proud of her new independence. When challenged by her family, she felt her value and worth being called into question. The price of confronting her family and living out her independence in a new way meant that she might have to separate herself from them or have them restructure how they were community for her. This was a price she was not sure she or they were ready to risk.

The pressures on Gloria were great. She did need a new community who could support her in the strong decisions she was making. In the end she needed to have a sense of her own worth enough to be able to risk the new behaviors that would bring her new strength and new ways to understand and value herself.

Spiritual care providers get stuck in this area when they buy people's commitments too easily and when they don't stick to helping people understand the cost and the price of a new life. Much like in the reconciliation process, some spiritual caregivers tend to downplay people's responsibility. The cost of new community and the cost of living in new ways can be a significant challenge. I suppose that this is partly attributable to the way spiritual caregivers have defined success in spiritual care. It has often been dependent on numbers: the number of people who come into our churches, the number of visits made, the size of budgets or new buildings.

Spiritual caregivers need to be clear about what new decisions for life cost. They need to have experienced those costs and risks themselves.

Vocation: A Call to Something beyond Ourselves

The last ritual area is vocation. Holy writings are filled with the call to step outside of our current situations and look at living in new ways. Holy writings are filled, as well, with what that means and the risks inherent in those calls.

In chapter 1 of the book of the prophet Jeremiah in Hebrew scriptures, God's call to Jeremiah is to go and challenge the people. A commission with plenty of risk. He could be beaten, thrown in jail, or ignored, but the call was still there and was issued again.

In Christian Scriptures the rich young ruler's question about how to gain eternal life and to be a true follower of God was answered with the huge price of selling all that he had and giving it to the poor. The young ruler grew sad as he tried to find a way that would still get him what he wanted without that full commitment.

Captured in those stories is the meaning of this area of vocation. Duffy writes in his book, "Service cannot ignore the specificity of our current life-stage and its crises. New commitments reshape our awareness of why and to whom we are sent. We recommit ourselves as we struggle to perceive the old and new gifts of others as well as our own gift."[6]

Each stage of our lives involves conflict and change. New commitments should result from the painful awareness of our current life stage and a new consciousness that "participation . . . is the only safeguard against a liturgical consumerism that cherishes relevant rituals but not the commitments they demand."[7]

6. Duffy, *Real Presence*, 148.
7. Duffy, *Real Presence*, 47.

When people are lost and striving for meaning outside of themselves, when they feel called, the theological/spiritual response is vocation, the sending out and setting apart.

a. The first stage is to recognize *a call from the community*, to have a sense of being touched by the Holy; called to find ourselves in a new way.

b. The second part of the process is the training stage. This is where we are equipped for this new life. The prophets were given words to speak. In marriage vows, in religious orders, in almost any new religious or spiritual community there is education and training about commitments.

c. There are *vows and commitments* to new life and behavior.

d. *Those who commit are sent out* by those they have imbued with wisdom and authority.

In each of the stages there is a sense of being called to something new that has a price. John, the architect who felt lost and uncertain in his work life, felt a call outside of himself to something better. He needed to have some image and understanding of what was possible in his job. He had an image early on in his career. The difficulties came when he got a clear understanding of the price involved in the commitment. People often get stuck when the price becomes clear.

The rich young ruler clearly felt the call and had heard Jesus speak. He had been around a community that had commitments to Jesus. He had some sense of the life commitments involved. He was stuck at the point where the vows were made clear and the commitment was required.

Spiritual care providers seem to get stuck when they have a fear of acting out of their own authority, to be people who call others to commitments beyond themselves. Those who have been trained in active listening skills tend to be cautious so as not to bring judgment or overstep bounds. This is not a particularly helpful stance with people who struggle with dis-ease in their vocation or meaning and direction. They need "callers." They need someone who will help them see what is beyond or to help them reach for something that is new. They need someone in their lives who has enough sense of their own authority to be one who also commissions and who sends out. Spiritual care providers, historically, seemed either to abuse the power and authority that was given to them or let that power and authority atrophy. Spiritual care providers need to be able to use the authority and to speak when people are lost and need to be found. They need to respond when people need to understand what commitment and vows are about. They need to be ready when people change the way they understand their calls in life.

The following diagram illustrates the stages under each ritual area.

Reconciliation

Acknowl-edgement	Confes-sion	Repen-tance	Making amends	Absolu-tion	

Community

Alone	Need	Confession	Decision	Welcome	
			for new life	to community	

Vocation

Call from community	Training	Vows	Commis-sion	Commit-ment	Send-ing

Summary

We all have all three types and needs as a part of us. Bringing them in balance is a goal of maturing and wholeness. There are times in major trauma when all three needs can be dis-eased; however, it is the primary need and type that defines us and most often determines our response to life and relationships.

Discovering the type of person we are dealing with and the need area that is disrupted and describing it spiritually and theologically ends the assessment task of the spiritual caregiver.

A common response as I present this material is that it takes a long time to work through this kind of process with each person. Spiritual caregivers who want to be taken seriously in the communities in which they work don't have the time not to be diacritics or assessors of type and need. They don't have time not to determine where they are going and a process they can communicate.

Like any diagnostician, the more spiritual caregivers work with the process, the quicker they come to informed opinions about people and their issues. When they begin to look for and see patterns, they eliminate certain possibilities because of the information observed. Those people who are inexperienced in some sort of assessment process will find their work with people less complicated and vague if they act responsibly as diacritics.

It is possible that the spiritual care provider may choose incorrectly. However, it is as important for the care provider to choose a course of response, to be able to analyze people's problems, as it is for a medical doctor to take some steps to act in the face of serious physical or mental illness. Spiritual care providers always need to position themselves to choose again or differently as the information changes or as new information is brought to light.

I believe that spiritual care response informed by spiritual care assessment is freeing. It helps avoid feelings of being overwhelmed by the variety of problems and issues before us. It puts some structure to what we do and gives us an ability to evaluate and have a sense of direction in our caregiving. It contains within it a sense of accomplishment and professional responsibility that can be enlivened in the face of a tremendous variety of people and situations.

Assessing people theologically or spiritually gives us back our language. Often, we have not been true to our roots and our strengths and our huge well-spring of resources for understanding people's dynamics. Assessing people in this manner takes seriously our theology and spirituality and its resources. In summary, the movement of types to needs to rituals follows:

Type	Need	Ritual
Achiever	Responsibility	Reconciliation
Giver	Self-worth	Community
Searcher	Meaning and direction	Vocation

SECTION 2

Spiritual Care Response
Doing and Being

THE GOAL OF SPIRITUAL care assessment is to inform the relationship of care and give direction to it.

The goal of spiritual care response is to create relationship through the embodiment of what we are trying to share. It focuses on who we are for people more than what we do for them.

One of the most difficult lessons that I had to learn in my caring for others was to trust the following:

What we do for people is only important as it serves who we are for them!

That statement is very difficult if we are oriented and trained to help people fix their problems. We can be effective at counseling technique or listening skills or problem solving or quoting holy writings, but if they do not serve who we are for people then we are not providing spiritual care. The key resource for spiritual care providers has always been who they are for people and how they are willing to be in relationship with them.

As you may have noticed in our ritual discussion, spiritual care assessment inherently presents us with a variety of ways in which to respond. Spiritual care response calls that variety forth and invites us to define our intentions and match them with behaviors. It challenges us to examine the interactions between the caregiver and the person receiving the care. Spiritual care response calls each person in the relationship to draw from their theology or spirituality and history.

If there is both science and art in spiritual care, then the science rests with assessment and the art with the response.

I believe spiritual care is a relationship that is intended to bring good news to where people live and to have it enliven them so that they live more abundantly. This means that when their need areas are dis-eased the spiritual care relationship can help create circumstances in which that dis-ease can be relieved or their yearning filled.

7

The Relationship Formula

IT TAKES TWO PEOPLE investing in a relationship to create a successful one. In spiritual care, it takes not only an informed caring response from the provider, but it also takes a response and commitment from the person receiving the care. That means a willingness on the person's part to recognize they are in need and a commitment to draw on resources available to them.

Spiritual care response provides someone outside of themselves to be with them in a way that will help them:

a. address things they haven't considered,

b. recognize their responsibility in their situations,

c. support them in their willingness to pay the price for new behavior,

d. and call them to new ways of being and relating.

One of the ways that has been helpful for me in thinking of the spiritual care relationship is the *relationship formula.* The three parts of that formula are the spiritual care response, the way the spiritual care provider transmits that response through being and doing, and the person's response. In formula, it appears below:

Transmission
SC response + person's response = balance in need

The formula involves both people. Both people have responsibility for their part in the relationship. The spiritual care provider's response and the ways that they pass on that response are the responsibility of the caregiver. How people respond, how they assess their situation and use their resources, is vital in determining whether the dis-ease will be quieted and the person will live as fully as possible.

Spiritual care providers need to be very intentional about the questions they ask about their caregiving. We need to ask ourselves how someone comes to take responsibility in relationships. How they come to value themselves, or how they find meaning and direction in their lives. Someone who has not learned to take responsibility in loving needs to be challenged. Persons who are struggling with self-worth need to be valued. People who avoid commitment and are searching need to be directed on a path.

Summary

Responsibility. The response called for from the spiritual caregiver for someone who is struggling with responsibility is challenge. The caregiver needs to understand that those with responsibility issues who need reconciliation most often get stuck at the point in the ritual of accepting that they are not taking their part of difficulties in relationships. Challenge then becomes the catalyst of moving them toward responsibility. This means not just voicing the challenge but being the authority who challenges.

Self-worth. For someone who is struggling with self-worth, the core response of the caregiver is to value the person and prepare them for a new community.

Commitment/meaning and purpose. The response for meaning and purpose is to be a caller to a commitment or higher purpose.

The above doesn't define in detail how we are going to communicate our responses to people, but it does declare the root and the intent of the care.

How spiritual caregivers define what is the core response has a lot to do with their own history, their theological and spiritual training, and needs. This is not just academic training or abstract theology but the lived-out spiritual beliefs that have become part of their lives. It is formed by the principles that people have chosen as important in their relationship with the Holy. It is formed by their definition of who they are as a spiritual caregiver and who they ought to be. It is formed by their views of humanity and the basic nature of humankind.

8

The Transmission of the Spiritual Care Response

THE TRANSMISSION OF THE spiritual care response is captured in embodiment and service.

I believe that there are two parts to the way we transmit our core response: service and embodiment, the things we do and who we are for people.

Spiritual care is an embodied act. Service gives form and practicality to it. The two are partners in bringing the Holy's presence to people.

In Christian Scripture in the story of the woman at the well, we watch Jesus enter this woman's world. He was not from her culture and shouldn't have been talking to her. He didn't stand outside her experience and point the way; he didn't just help her to come to insight into her situation, although that was part of it. He became a new community for her, and she felt valued because of it.

The service aspects of spiritual care in transmitting the Holy's presence are crucial to our relationships with people. Helping people through crisis, putting them in touch with people who can help them, giving them new ideas, helping them try on new behavior and express their feelings, helping them define their problems, praying with people, and sharing holy writings—all these activities are important in our relationships.

These actions, however, are always reflective of who we are with people. In Christianity, Jesus knew that who he was was more important than what he did. He constantly turned people's questions away from the miraculous happenings that surrounded him to the message. He was the message. People connected their faith and their understandings of God to the way he was and not just to what he said or did.

We, as spiritual care providers, embody the Holy's presence for those Achievers needing responsibility and reconciliation by being a reconciled person who has taken responsibility in relationships and who is free to challenge them to do the same. We do it for Givers in need of self-worth by being a new community who can hold up their worth and create support. We do it for the Searchers with meaning and purpose needs by being a caller to a new life.

What this means is that who we are and what we do are informed by our spiritual care assessment, our understanding of which ritual process is a part of people's lives, and by committing ourselves to the appropriate core response.

The tendency for spiritual caregivers in transmitting response is very much like the earlier tendency in spiritual care assessment, to keep things general. The two parts of transmitting response, service and embodiment, should be specific. It is not enough to say a person needs community or reconciliation. We need to be specific about who we are as community and a reconciled person ourselves. Our responses should be in tune with people's type and needs and where they are in the ritual process. We are called to respond in one way in our relationships if people are having trouble bringing themselves to judgment, another way if they are having trouble believing they are forgiven, and yet another way if they are struggling with what amends might be for their situations, and another way if they need training or a call to new purpose.

Jack, whose wife had committed him to a state hospital, was being cared for by a priest who was his physical and emotional opposite. The priest assessed the patient's dis-eased need as self-worth. The man needed a new community, a new concept of himself that would allow his own ability and pain to be a part of who he was. The priest came to understand that the embodiment being called for was to be truly who he was; a vulnerable, sensitive, caring man, and free to let that show. This was difficult for the priest in relationship with a man who made fun of him, his commitments, and his stature. He was called, in this situation, not only to accept himself but to use who he was and to invite Jack into a new understanding of himself. The service that flowed out of that embodied commitment was the priest's sharing of his vulnerability and fears while not feeling he was diminished by the sharing. These two men learned a tremendous amount from each other and the healing that took place was remarkable.

Janet needed to find a way out of blaming others for her problems and standing as a victim in whatever happened to her. The spiritual caregiver with her began by understanding that she was an Achiever who needed to begin to take responsibility. The chaplain saw her resistance to challenges and, while not shying away from the challenger role, began to help Janet discover where she could gain power in new ways. It was not a frontal challenge but a subtle way to approach her with ways she could take responsibility for her life. The chaplain did not yield to her victim side nor accept a role as a victimizer but was someone who held new possibilities for her without taking away her power.

John, the architect, had a minister of his congregation who was able to be the one who supported his call to a new vocation. He helped him sort through options and make commitments to new ways of working. In addition, he understood the cost of changing for John and he and the congregation were a community of support during the process.

The principle of spiritual care upon which all of this is based is the belief that *spiritual care is not a spectator activity*. The healing took place within the relationship. The caregiver is not called to stand outside people's worlds and their experience and point the way for them or offer for them an echoed response of their own words. We are called to involve ourselves in their lives. To do so we need to be willing to walk through the valley of the shadow, their shadows and our own.

These journeys are not easy. If we are willing to take them, however, like the people in the previous example, we can find healing not only for those whom we serve but also for ourselves. Spiritual care is most often limited because people are either unwilling or unable to see themselves taking these kinds of journeys with others. Since the beginning of time, people have had holy people with them so that when crisis struck, they had someone who was willing to be there with them, to walk through the frightening times, and to stand with them in front of the Holy.

Parker Palmer in his wonderful little book *Let Your Life Speak* describes this process as he quotes Annie Dillard: "If we ride those monsters all the way down, we break through to something precious—to 'the unified field, our complex and inexplicable caring for each other,' to the community we share beneath the broken surface of our lives. Good leadership comes from people who have penetrated their own inner darkness and arrived at the place where we are at one with one another."[1]

Recently in a health center, one of the chaplains walked into a code situation. The patient was clearly dying. There was a minister in the room with the family. The minister looked uncomfortable, searching for the right words to say. The family voiced their concern again and again. "Reverend, please don't leave us now, please stay with us." They felt the minister's discomfort and asked for what they wanted from him: his presence, a reminder of God's presence.

Spiritual care is a symbolic act whether we like it or not, whether we feel capable or not. We stand in for the Holy at key points in people's lives. Those may be celebrations or crises, but we are called to be present. People value that presence whether they value us as people or whether we think we are capable. This role as the presence of the Holy reminds us and the people we serve that we are not alone. It is our greatest resource as spiritual care providers.

1. Palmer, *Let Your Life Speak*, 80–81.

When I was a young chaplain, the director of the department called and said he wanted me to go to the surgery waiting area to meet with a neurosurgeon so that he could tell the family that their family member had died during surgery. This surgeon was notorious for not being good with families. True to form he came out and said to the family, "We did everything we could but he died." He then turned and left. I was stunned, and the wife and sister of the patient were stunned. The questions began quickly centered around *why*. "Why did this happen to such a good man?" "He was a Sunday school teacher; he loved us and people around him, who does that surgeon think he is?" To me the wife said, "Why did God do this? Tell us." I didn't do very well that day. None of my attempted answers helped. They got angrier as I tried to answer. Finally, they refused to pray with me and said, "You need to leave right now."

Two weeks later, in the very long main hallway of the hospital, I saw the wife coming toward me. With great courage I tried the locked door to the social worker's office. Stuck, I turned to face the woman. "Chaplain Kenny (*oh no, she remembered my name*) I'm glad I'm able to talk to you. I wanted to say thank you to you. I don't remember what you said to us the day my husband died, but the fact you came and you were there was so important to us. You were wonderful." Huh? Wow, what just happened?

I learned important lessons that day, and they have sustained me through the years. I was so thankful that these two women were my teachers in an awful time for them.

In many health care systems, a professional spiritual care provider is one of a few caregivers who can walk into a patient's room without a physician's order. We can step into places in people's lives without an invitation or specific request to offer our presence and service. We are even able to do this with people who are not part of an organized religion or do not see themselves as people of a Holy Other.

This is a tremendous and holy responsibility. People are willing to excuse our stumbles or awkward caring because they value caring in any form. This ought to give us a significant sense of freedom in the ways that we relate to people. The spirit of the Holy working through us can create good out of some very imperfect models and responses.

Because of opportunities to be present, we are called to make the most out of our care and personal resources. How we transmit this message to people is most often limited by our understanding of ourselves and our definitions of ministry: those things we think we cannot do or should not do in our relationships with people. It is also limited by some practical considerations such as time, physical or emotional limitations, or lack of experience in particular life situations.

It is most limited, however, by how we understand ourselves and the principles that have grown out of that understanding.

In a case conference, with several very competent spiritual caregivers, it became apparent that there were many different ideas about how to respond to the person who was the focus of the meeting. As we talked, some basic principles about what we thought spiritual care could do for others became clear. A couple of caregivers were not willing to challenge a person because they believed that spiritual caregivers should not risk hurting someone who came to them for help. They felt that one of the challenging ways suggested would violate this principle of their care.

Another opinion that emerged was that it was not appropriate for the spiritual caregiver to risk becoming emotionally involved with the person. The proponent of this was particularly wary of transference and countertransference and the limitations of spiritual caregivers to handle such dynamics. The emphasis of this caring was that the person could be given insight to understand the situation intellectually and thus make a new choice without the caregiver risking being enmeshed in the situation.

In an ongoing class I was teaching on integrative medicine and spirituality these issues came to the forefront. We had talked about spiritual assessment in depth and the class wanted to know, "What do we do now?" There were several disciplines represented in the room. They included chaplains, massage therapists, reiki practitioners, nurses, and physicians.

Section 2: Spiritual Care Response

One of the nurses particularly wanted information and had concerns about how the care was done. To teach the principles I often used role play. There were two choices for the person in the role of receiving care. The participants could make up a situation they wanted to talk about or they could talk about a situation that was real in their life. The second person would then try to help. On occasion others would "tap in" to take over the care and try a different approach. The nurse was concerned about getting "too personal" with patients and didn't see how it could help. With significant courage she volunteered to be the care receiver and chose to talk about a real situation in her life. She shared that she had not talked about the topic with anyone and began slowly. What started slowly became an amazing moment of healing and teaching. People cared about her and were with her as she struggled and shared. At the end she talked about how much she felt cared for and how much freer she felt from the sharing of her story in a caring community. She understood firsthand what spiritual care could do in a short period of time when there was care given and when the care receiver was willing to risk sharing and receiving the care.

The difficulty with the two approaches discussed earlier was that, while they were intended to minimize risk, they had the effect of keeping the caregiver distant from the person and their key issues. I question the assumption that challenge would hurt more than caution would, or that intellectual distance diminishes the possibility of transference and countertransference. Risk and personal involvement are natural, inevitable consequences of embodying the Holy's presence for people in the difficult places of their lives.

Walking with people into the corners of their lives often calls us to go places that we have not travelled to ourselves. We may be reluctant to journey through dark places in our own lives and then, ironically, be called to walk the journey there as the caregiver with someone else. How effectively can we care for someone else on their journey if we have not walked and understood our own?

How can we ask someone in our care to live in a new way with its price if we have refused to pay our price for walking in a new way?

As spiritual care providers we must be aware of our own "stuck places," those places in our personalities, our motivations, our behaviors in relationship that cringe or flee before examination.

The priest in the previous example experienced considerable personal risk being vulnerable with a man who had ridiculed his sensitivity. The priest had been challenged on that most of his life, particularly as a young boy. He had struggles with his sexuality for many years. He had been told that he was too effeminate. To set his fear aside and show his vulnerability met the needs of the person and placed him at risk and exacted a price. It was precisely his willingness to take the risk that made a difference in Jack's life and helped him move to a different understanding of himself. The priest finally saw that his vulnerability was not something to fight; it was a significant resource in his spiritual care. He could use his vulnerability to help others reach into themselves, to find self-knowledge rooted in new possibilities.

The sacrifice on the priest's part allowed him to let go of destructive self-images from his childhood and empowered Jack to release the vulnerable self he kept hidden behind a false "macho" exterior. This is the true nature of sacrifice in spiritual care, and it requires commitment to the truth of oneself in relationship to another. The rewards of this sacrifice are healing for both the giver and the person being cared for.

Sarah, the spiritual caregiver who could not challenge people who appeared hurt and vulnerable, had great difficulty integrating judgment into her spiritual care. It was not so much a matter of whether the person could handle being challenged, but whether Sarah could handle giving a challenge. She felt she could not hurt another the way she had been hurt as a child. The sacrifice Sarah was called upon to make was to let go of an image of herself as the wounded child, an image which she constantly projected onto the vulnerable other person. Sarah's sacrifice meant committing herself to coming into the present, placing the anger and blame where it belonged, recognizing other people's inner child as distinctly

Section 2: Spiritual Care Response

their own and not hers. For survivors of abuse this is an ongoing challenge. Sarah struggled with this throughout her spiritual care. Therapy and training helped as Sarah gradually began to broaden her concept of spiritual care and found it helpful to connect the concepts of spiritual care assessment, the ritual process, and spiritual care response. Using this model gave her some internal distance from her own dynamics and helped her sort out what she was projecting onto the other person.

If doing spiritual care has sacrifice, perhaps changing our patterns and changing our ways of caring is an even greater sacrifice. But for many of us it is essential. When our theological and spiritual principles and our relationships with the Holy have not been examined and become entangled with our definition of spiritual care, our power to help others becomes limited.

The following chart shows the core responses and basic embodiment called for in response to each type and need.

Achiever

Response—caregiver	Transmission	Response—care receiver	Outcome
Challenge	(embodiment)	Responsibility	Reconciliation
	Reconciler		
	(service)		

Giver

Response—caregiver	Transmission	Response—care receiver	Outcome
Value	Community	I have value	Self-worth

84

Searcher

Response—caregiver	Transmission	Response—care receiver	Outcome
Direction	Caller	Commitment	Meaning and direction

Spiritual care response should not be formed by a definition of spiritual care that arises out of a rigid approach or our comfort zones, but by an assessment of people and where they are in their own process. There is a great value in following an objective process based on relationship truths and congruent with theology or spirituality and training. It aids in understanding our own and other's interpersonal dynamics. It gives spiritual care providers an objective process of evaluation with which to examine their own responses as well as assess the person's need.

9

Common Problems in Spiritual Care

I'VE TALKED EARLIER ABOUT the problems with choosing one style that fits all. The relationship formula on the above charts demonstrates that the spiritual care response needs to be matched with the way the response is transmitted to the person and is in response to their type and need.

There are common problems inherent in spiritual care relationships, which can be made to work more smoothly using this model.

An example is the spiritual care provider who assesses the person as needing self-worth, then spends most of their time talking to the person about where they have sinned and what they need to do to get themselves right with the Holy One and line up with what the religious group teaches. These caregivers operate out of rigid spiritual care styles that hold the other person and their problems secondary to the caregiver's own comfort level.

Another common spiritual care style is seen in those who assess persons as needing to know they are loved or valued, and then proceed to ask question after question to help them come to insight. The value and love get lost.

The third approach is seen in the spiritual care provider who, no matter what the need, is the good listener and feeds back what people say.

Intentionally matching spiritual care response with the assessed need of the person can go a long way in helping us bring healing to people in meaningful ways. The priest working with Jack in an earlier example had decided the main dis-eased need was self-worth. He had decided the macho man attitude was a cover for basic inferiority problems. His plans were to work with Jack's attitudes and ways of approaching others. He did this, early on in the relationship, by asking the man a lot of questions about himself and his background. He often asked him why he did certain things or approached people in particular ways. He tried to model behavior that would help Jack get in touch with his feelings by confronting him and sharing his own irritation with him when Jack expressed some of his macho attitudes. This approach was consistent with the behavior modification methods that the floor staff were using with Jack. I asked the priest whether he felt his behavior with Jack matched his goal of helping him feel a greater sense of self-worth. He struggled with his answer, looked over his responses to Jack, and finally said no. In fact, he realized that his responses probably contributed to undermining Jack's attitude about himself. His spiritual care responses had been transmitting the belief that Jack was not valued unless he changed.

Having admitted this, the priest was not at all sure he wanted to take the steps he needed to help this person feel valued. He was not sure he wanted to learn ways to accept Jack and model vulnerability for someone he saw as a "jerk."

I did not ask the priest to set aside his own feelings about the man but to use them and make them a part of the relationship. It was important for the priest to consider what it meant to accept his own fears and vulnerability. He needed to experience them as a part of himself and risk sharing them with another to find that they would be acceptable. It was important for the priest to know that he didn't have to set his irritation aside. He didn't have to be somebody he was not. Instead, he was being challenged to respond in ways that were congruent with his own spiritual care assessment and good sense about how people learn about vulnerability and acceptance.

He was faced with clear decisions about whether he wanted to try on new behaviors that he knew would help this man. If he chose not to respond, then at least this decision was a conscious one. He would no longer unconsciously be punishing Jack for the ridicule he had experienced and the anger he felt.

Valerie's story is another example of the need to do a good assessment and match the spiritual care response with it. Valerie had been going to see her mother every Wednesday at 2:00 p.m. for several years. The Wednesday visits were intended to help her mother, who lived alone, prepare her grocery list for the week and do some heavy cleaning. The daughter would then do the grocery shopping and any other shopping that seemed to be necessary for the rest of the week. One Wednesday, however, Valerie decided to do some shopping of her own before going to visit her mother. Her shopping trip made her an hour late getting to her mother's house.

Valerie walked in the front door, called to her mother, and, not getting an answer, figured her mother was probably trying to punish her for being late. Feeling irritated and guilty, Valerie strode into the kitchen. Her mother lay dead on the kitchen floor. Later the autopsy report set the time of death at 2:00 p.m., the time Valerie would have arrived at the house had she not gone shopping for herself. The minister at Valerie's church helped with the funeral preparations and cared for the family in their grief.

Two months after the funeral Valerie's husband called the minister and asked him to visit with Valerie. He felt her grieving was going beyond what was appropriate. In talking with Valerie, the minister continued to support her by giving her an opportunity to express her grief and her feelings about her mother.

During this conversation, she shared her guilt over being late. Had she arrived on time, she said, her mother might still be alive. She might have gotten her to the hospital in time to save her. The minister felt that her self-recrimination was a natural part of the grief process and assured Valerie that there really wasn't anything she could have done. It was just an unfortunate coincidence that her mother died at the time she ordinarily would have arrived.

Valerie left appearing to feel better. The minister felt she had heard her and supported her in her grief. A couple of months later the husband returned to the minister and again asked for help. Valerie had become seriously depressed. She had stopped taking good care of herself. She was clearly not getting any better and not moving through the grieving process.

The minister referred Valerie to a psychologist in her congregation and helped her make the initial appointment. The psychologist also assessed the situation as an intense grief reaction centered around inappropriate guilt. He counseled Valerie for six months. His approach with her was much like the minister's: He attempted to show her that her guilt, although appropriate early in the grief experience, was no longer appropriate. He affirmed that she did not bear any responsibility for her mother's death.

The minister continued to talk with Valerie while she was seeing the psychologist. The minister brought the problem to me at a pastoral counseling seminar. The first task was to help the minister assess Valerie's type and dis-eased need. The need was assessed as self-worth, and therefore supportive care seemed to be the best way to go.

After some discussion about whether Valerie in fact had something to be guilty of, the minister reassessed her as a possible Achiever with reconciliation issues. Valerie had not accepted responsibility for being angry with her mother and being intentionally late. Telling her she had nothing to feel guilty about fed her own denial and did not help her move toward forgiveness. The minister decided to look a little more closely at Valerie's guilt. She visited with her and asked her to talk a little bit more about her guilt and asked specifically why she was feeling guilty about her mother's death.

Valerie immediately began to talk about being late that day. The minister kept the ritual process of reconciliation in mind as she journeyed with Valerie through her activities that afternoon.

She asked her why she had decided to go shopping instead of getting to her mother's house at her usual time. The story began to unfold. Valerie went shopping for herself knowing she would be late. It was an unnecessary shopping trip. The minister asked again why she had made the trip at that time. Suddenly angry feelings, guilt, and tears began to flow. Valerie explained that her mother had always been a demanding, irritable old woman; she had never thanked her for the many years Valerie had cared for her. So, that day, Valerie decided she could come a little later than usual and let her mother learn the value of those visits.

This reflects the deep subtlety of communication and dynamics in relationships that go beyond presence and spoken words. Initially Valerie's need was mis-assessed, but the minister adjusted this as Valerie's grief seemed prolonged. After assessing her as needing responsibility and reconciliation, the minister then intentionally tried to match her behavior with understanding where the woman might be stuck in the reconciliation process.

The minister did not dismiss Valerie's feelings of guilt as lightly as she had earlier. Her assessment allowed Valerie to explore her own responsibility for the situation. It was not easy for this minister to allow Valerie to stay in her pain and guilt. Her ministry style was often supportive of people and avoided confrontation. In this situation, her confrontation with Valerie was built on a nurturing relationship. She had the advantage of having already worked with her and knowing that previous reassurance had not helped her move out of her grief and guilt. This time the minister was prepared to embody a woman friend, a spiritual care reconciler, who was willing to hear her confession. In her embodiment the spiritual care provider risked making Valerie angry. She was prepared to embody a reconciled person who could risk provoking anger and was still lovable. She embodied for Valerie a person with whom Valerie could be angry and express that anger safely, as opposed to acting her anger out in a passive-aggressive manner, as she had with her mother. She was offered a new way of dealing with conflict in her relationships. We will discuss later how Valerie responded to this kind of care.

After hearing a seminar entitled "Do People Choose Their Illnesses," Dorothy came up to me and asked to talk. We talked about her illnesses. She wanted to look at why and how she might be contributing to them. I had never had someone be that direct with a request like this. It showed significant courage or pain.

She described having back problems and pains in her legs for approximately four years. She had seen physicians and chiropractors. She eventually had surgery, which had helped some of her pain. She had followed the prescribed exercise program faithfully since the operation. She recognized that the pain flared up when she was under significant stress.

We set up a contract to be focused specifically around helping her explore where relationship issues might have contributed to illness. Dorothy was a woman in her thirties. She was self-motivated, curious, and intelligent. We talked about her history, and she said she was the oldest child in a family of six. The family was very close and strongly Catholic. She talked about the strong values she had learned in the family and how they had become an integral part of her life. She was unmarried and actively committed to one of the helping professions. When I asked which of her relationships was the most stressful to her, she began to talk about her relationship with her parents. Her father had cancer, and she had recently realized that he was an alcoholic. She saw her mother as an enabler, unwilling to face her father's alcoholism. Dorothy was the main caretaker not only for her parents but also for some of her siblings.

She felt the relationship between her mother and father, and her father's problems, were a burden she was forced to carry. We talked about whether it was necessary for her to take all the responsibility. We looked at whether her other siblings or a parish pastor might help share the burden.

We brainstormed ways she might begin sharing the responsibility and listed ways to behave differently with her parents. Soon it was apparent to me that Dorothy had other issues troubling her that she was not sharing with me. When I told her about my sense of this she hesitantly began to talk about her relationship with a married man. I asked her about her social life generally and whether she saw herself as a person who could commit to a relationship or would choose to be married. She said that she would but that she had not been dating much. She had not met many men who interested her. She said she had been trying to make herself available. I asked how that was possible if she was involved with a married man. We talked about the relationship. She said that he planned to leave his wife but couldn't do so immediately. He valued his relationship with Dorothy and didn't want to lose her. Dorothy was clearly embarrassed to talk about the relationship. She realized it was not good for her. She continued to claim that she was "available for something better if it came along."

Gradually the emotional reality of her claims became clear to her and Dorothy admitted she was afraid of an emotional commitment. She also came to grips with how her behavior was like the enabling behavior she criticized about her mother.

We ended our work together with an evaluation period. We had isolated the two major stress points in her life: the relationship with her parents and the relationship with the married man. She and I both felt she had made significant steps toward lessening the burden with her parents.

She was not ready to leave the relationship with the married man or even restructure it in a way that would help her meet her needs. She was committed to staying in the relationship, believing that he would eventually leave his wife. When I asked her why she had trouble leaving the relationship, she said, "He has such a good heart and he needs me." We parted with her understanding that this would continue to be a stressful relationship for her, not only because of the secrecy required but because it violated her religious and personal values.

My assessment of Dorothy was a Giver whose dis-eased need area was self-worth. The dis-ease had acted itself out in some physical ailments, particularly in her back and legs. She was the oldest child, and it was hard for her to give up responsibilities in relationships, even when she saw they were not helpful to her or others. It was hard for her to claim her own needs in relationships or to speak up for herself and say no when it was appropriate. She was a nurturer and intimately acquainted with self-sacrifice, even when it jeopardized her own health and values.

If we had continued our conversations, I would have seen myself not only helping her see the connections and gain insight into her situation, but I would have built on being a new community for her calling her to live in a new way. I felt she was stuck in the ritual process at the point of deciding for new life. She certainly had insight into where she was stuck as well as insight into her dynamics. It was now time for her to choose for herself. She needed to choose a healthy and abundant life. She was willing to pay the price in her relationship with her parents but not willing to pay the price in her relationship with the married man. Because her diseased need was self-worth, embodying community for her meant valuing her even though she was making decisions that abdicated her responsibility for herself. At the close of our relationship, I tried to embody someone who would care for her, give her the freedom to make her own choices, and not care any less because her choices were not what I would have chosen.

10

The Care Receiver's Response

THE PERSON'S RESPONSE TO spiritual care offered is dependent, in large measure, on the person's type and their patterns of interaction and decisions made about what's important in life. It is also dependent on how the person sees the Holy one and their theological or spiritual assumptions made about living. It is also greatly affected by which need area is dis-eased and where the person is in the ritual process.

Most of us have a bank of resources and limitations that can be triggered when significant life events happen to us. Our ability to decide for a new life is largely dependent upon what kind of balance exists between our resources and our limitations. Our resources generally come from having had people in our life who cared about us unconditionally and who gave us some firm structure in which to set our limitations and know our boundaries.

In the case of some people I've worked with, their histories show they received little appreciation, love, care, and boundary setting in their childhoods. Positive responses from those who cared for them were hard to come by, although each time someone cared their resource bank grew. It is true that caring, self-aware spiritual care providers, who understand the world of the people for whom they are caring, can help balance these ledgers.

In assessing how responsive a person is likely to be to our care, there are five signs to look for:

a. The ability to acknowledge there is a problem

b. The ability to ask for and receive help

c. A willingness to take responsibility for their action

d. A willingness to pay the price of the changes for new life

e. A commitment to live out the new behavior

These five indicators seem to be the abilities that are captured in each of the areas in the ritual process that allows people to move on to quiet their dis-ease. They reflect the places in the process where people get stuck.

a. Achievers require an ability to acknowledge problems and accept responsibility.

b. Givers have self-worth needs.

c. Searchers have meaning and direction needs.

All require a willingness to pay the price of new life.

Keeping an eye out for the indicators in the ritual processes can not only help the spiritual caregiver know how things are moving along, but it can also inform the responses the caregiver makes and may change the assessment of the person. The phrases used and the behaviors lived out give us indications of whether the person is willing to work on quieting the dis-ease in their need areas.

For Jack, the change required was for him to see himself as a vulnerable human being who could get in touch with his pain and share it with others. It meant acknowledging there was a problem. It meant changing his social life. Being able to share pain and vulnerability would exact a price from him but it would also welcome him into new community possibilities. The priest began seeing changes in Jack. He started talking more about his feelings and sharing painful stories. He was less inclined to blame his wife for his problems and began to accept responsibility for some of them. The hospital staff made mention of the fact that his visits with his wife were better. He was seen in tears with her. This was very different from an earlier meeting where he was combative and arrogant.

The architect, John, who was struggling with meaning and direction was clear that the commitment he was being asked to adopt was the place that he needed to pay attention to. He had been able to identify the problem, at least in general terms, and had been able to ask for help. It was now up to him to decide whether to pay the price with his company and with his family. He started the process by talking to both groups. Neither liked the idea, and the price became clearer. The spiritual care provider was encouraged by these signs, but he knew that exploring how the people in John's life felt about the changes was only the beginning. Making specific plans to start his own business was the necessary step, and that was difficult, but it happened and John found a purpose to commit to.

Valerie, who was on a shopping trip when her mother died, did make the decision to move on, and it was captured in one phrase that she shared with her spiritual care provider. It turned her whole situation around. That phrase was "I guess I was paying my mother back that day when I didn't go on time." It started the process of reconciliation. Acknowledging that she had responsibility for being angry with her mother and acting it out with shopping freed her to move on to forgiveness and absolution. She had been able, in the previous months, to identify the problem and to ask for help, but she had not been willing to claim that there had been some anger between her and her mother. She had been too willing to accept the easy grace that had been offered her. The emotional reality was that she felt responsible and was trapped by her anger at her mother. Claiming her anger began her steps toward renewed healing.

11

Change

CHANGE IS POSSIBLE WHEN the pain of staying the same is equal to or greater than the pain of changing.

Each of the people in the previous examples faced a decision about change. The steps of change are the steps of the ritual process. For some, the decision to change meant taking responsibility, for some it meant accepting anger or forgiveness, and for others it meant giving up old ways and accepting new ones.

What needs to happen to make those decisions possible? We need to change our basic understanding of ourselves expressed in the ways we define life and relationships. What is the catalyst of change? It can be the embodied presence of the Holy, through a caregiver willing to be at the point where change needs to occur. It can also be the point when the pain of staying the same is equal to or greater than the pain of changing.

It seems that human beings change with great difficulty. When exterior forces create enough pain, we will move to a new place. When there is a caregiver who cares enough to be present to us at the point of our need, we can create a new vision of what is possible for us and a new vision of who we are in relationship to the Holy.

People need to be able to come to the place where they can say, "I am different; I see the world and the Holy differently" and have that be reality for them, if they are to quiet the dis-ease in their need areas. The Giver needs to move from saying, "I am at fault; I cannot change." The Achiever needs to be able to move from "You are at fault, I won't change." The Searcher needs to be able to move from "I am lost and don't know what to change."

My wife, Ruth, and I have worked hard on our relationship. The issues hit a crisis point several years ago as she struggled with her own self-worth and independence and discovered considerable repressed anger. I had always seen myself as a champion of people's rights. It was a significant struggle for me to see myself as someone who had contributed to oppressing my wife. I said, when challenged, that through the years I had encouraged her to work outside the home and to continue her graduate education. I did not own the countless ways that I had not fostered her growth, or that I gave on the one hand but held back on the other, as if my permission or lack of it was the issue.

As we struggled and fought through these times, I continued to defend myself. Her anger increased and the distance in our relationship grew. It was only at the point when I could hear that, whether I understood it or not, she felt oppressed that the relationship improved. My oppression and society's oppression led her to make choices that she ordinarily would not have made. She felt forced into situations in which she felt she had no power. The changes occurred for me through several converging events.

At about the time our relationship was hitting a crisis point, my mother died. Four months later, Ruth and I separated. We both continued therapy and I went on a six-day retreat. Those are the facts. Those things which aided my hearing and coming to new understanding were seeing and feeling Ruth's pain and great struggle with her commitment to me and her desire for inner freedom. Therapy and friends who listened to, cared for, and challenged me helped. A directed retreat, led by a trusted friend who walked with me through my grief, helped.

My pain and my experience of Ruth's pain created a situation where the pain of staying the same became greater than the pain of changing. My friends, and especially my retreat director, cared for me at the point of my need into a new vision of who I was in my relationship with God and others. The most significant surprise was an insight that I was more committed to commitment and achievement than I was, at times, to people. This kind of commitment was experienced by Ruth, and I assume by others, as oppression. This insight was unexpected and came as I was grieving my mother. It helped change my world.

When I could own the insight and take responsibility for it, I was different in my relationships. It was an experience that brought me new life and freedom and helped renew our marriage.

Nothing much is possible for those who say, "I am not at fault," or "I am at fault and I can't change," or "I'm lost and don't know what to change," whether we are talking about ourselves, our lives, or our relationship with someone else. Nothing is possible until we can say, "I am worth something; I can change." Or "it is my responsibility to change." Or "I can commit to a new path."

We live in a world with pressures from a variety of places: pressures forced by poverty, wealth, power or lack of it, by race and culture, or by multiple responsibilities for family and career. We are often placed in the middle of contrasting, conflicting forces that pull us in different directions. They may leave us confused and uncertain. "I cannot find my way" needs to change to "I see the options; I can feel the strength and have been helped to gather the courage to take the steps that will lead me in a different way."

The spiritual caregiver needs to know the journey and provide opportunities to create a new vision. She or he needs to believe in the worth of people and their ability to change, and she or he needs to be able to stay with persons in conflict until they claim their responsibilities in relationships.

Change is not easy, either for the person doing the changing or for the caregiver aiding the process. Caregivers need to know that their responsibility stops with their assessment and an informed response.

There are times when ministers stop too early in their relationships with people making decisions to change. Crisis often brings with it windows of opportunities for us to reevaluate deep-seated values and personal understandings of life and the Holy. While the spiritual caregiver needs to be ready to enter the conflict through a call for responsibility, valuing the fearful, and calling for new directions, it is important to remember that *change is the person's choice and responsibility, not ours.*

Spiritual caregivers need to explore their beliefs about change. How attached are they to seeing this person change? How invested are they in their own ideas about how this person should change? How do they feel about people who refuse to change or who change without regard to boundaries? They need to be able to identify when people are committed and struggling with the effects of new behavior as opposed to making a firm decision not to change. People can change, if the spiritual caregiver is willing to risk walking the path with them.

Understanding why changing may be difficult, where the resistance to change resides, how it is formed, and how it affects the caregiving relationship is the topic of the next chapter of this book.

12

Formation of Types, Needs, and Spiritual Agreements

WHILE IT IS TRUE that we have all three types and needs operating in us, we operate out of a primary type and need that is formed by our life experience. There are principles and spiritual agreements that are formed from them. A good part of what makes change difficult is that our spiritual agreements or covenants with the Holy are guardians of and live where our needs are yearned for or become dis-eased.

Spiritual agreements are life principles and values from which decisions are made and relationships built. What makes them different from life scripts or other ways to describe them from a sociological or psychological way is that they come from and are defined by our relationship with the Holy. In the ritual process, that means our spiritual agreements live where we are most likely to be stuck.

These principles are spelled out in my book *Promise of The Soul: Identifying and Healing Your Spiritual Agreements.* I talk about the covenants, or spiritual agreements, that are created out of our life experiences and families of origin. These agreements to a large measure determine how we are in the world and relationships and how we respond when in crisis. They live at the point of our needs and are the guardians of how we respond. When we attach our spirituality and theology to our beliefs about the world and our place in it, their influence on us grows exponentially.

When we decide to encourage people to change or to look at their spiritual agreements that affect their changing, we need to know that we are in the arena of the Holy. When spiritual agreements are challenged, it feels as if our relationship with the Holy is being challenged.

The spiritual care relationship is a dynamic relationship. In the relationship formula it takes both people responding and interacting to quiet the dis-ease in people's needs.

The way spiritual caregivers transmit their response and the way persons receive that response and respond in turn are affected by people's type and needs and the spiritual agreements formed from them. How the person responds to the spiritual caregiver and the way the caregiver offers help flows out of the way they see the world and the spiritual agreements that have been formed to make sense of it.

The experience of Sarah, the chaplain who did not want to hurt anyone like she had been hurt (her spiritual agreement), led her to form concepts of care that were in line with this unconscious, unexamined spiritual principle. She assessed most people as having self-worth problems and needing support and affirmation. She avoided assessing people as Achievers with responsibility issues. She knew if that assessment was made then she would have to include some judgment or confrontation in her relationship with the people she was trying to help.

She was confronted with the contradictions in her principles when people told her that she often appeared challenging, aloof, and unwelcoming, especially early in relationships. Her spiritual agreement made her cautious with certain types of people.

I was called one day by a nursing supervisor on one of the floors where Sarah was chaplain. The nurse was very concerned because one of the patients Sarah had been seeing was crying each time Sarah left the room. The concern was multilayered. The nurse did not know Sarah well and Sarah did not often talk to the nurses or consult with them. They found her curt and distant.

I talked first to Sarah and then to the patient. Sarah talked about her relationship with the nurses and with other professional staff with whom she had worked. She did not see them as people who needed God's presence or help but as people who contributed to the oppression of others. When this dynamic took over, her stored up anger created the aloofness that the nurses experienced.

Sarah felt that she had been gentle and nurturing with the patient. The patient had begun to share some sexual abuse she had experienced as a child.

I visited the patient and asked her how she felt her relationship with the chaplain had been. She said that Sarah had been helpful in confronting her. "I need it, but it's been hard, and it makes me cry," the patient shared. When I asked how she would describe Sarah she said, "She's tough but has been helpful. She certainly wasn't comforting, but it helped."

This is a typical situation, in capsule form, of how the dynamics of a caregiver's unexamined spiritual agreement can affect their relationships. It is not at all unusual that spiritual caregivers' feelings about themselves affect their relationships. What is important is to know when they are connected to our spiritual agreements and how that affects our relationships.

It is important for spiritual care providers to have some sense of who they are in relationships, what their patterns are, and what influences the way they interact with others. It is vitally important to examine their theological or spiritual principles and their effect on their care.

In much the same way that feelings and ways of relating to others are subsumed under the theology or spirituality of the spiritual agreements of the caregiver, the same is true for those who are receiving the care. Persons relating to a minister filter a lot of what they say and tailor how they react depending on their spiritual agreements. It does not matter how rough-hewn or underdeveloped the spirituality. It does not matter if the person has no spirituality. All of us have principles by which we try to live, whatever we call them.

I have found that no matter how little experience a person has had with religious groups and their representatives, relating to a spiritual care provider causes them to draw from whatever experience happens to be in their history. The old axiom that "there is no atheist in a foxhole" has some truth to it whenever people are in crisis.

I have had some very meaningful times with people who have told me in the beginning of our relationship that they did not believe in God, did not want any part of church, and could not understand why a minister would want to come see them. When I wasn't thrown out of the room and the person had some curiosity about why I was there, some very important discussions about the meaning of life, the meaning of their illness, and their struggles with their own death resulted. I think they found value in talking to someone trying to help them. In their time of crisis, they could find comfort talking with a person in whom they perceived the Holy's symbolic or real presence. Even with those who asked me to leave, they found some control during uncontrollable situations. Spiritual caregivers are one of the few people in a hospital the patient can ask to leave. A valuable role.

Negative ideas of the Holy's role in people's illness can have a significant impact on their health. Reeducating or rescripting people's spiritual agreements can go a long way to easing people's burdens and aid in a healthier outlook on life.

The spiritual caregiver above had very different patterns of relationship with those she considered as vulnerable than she had with those she saw as authorities. People in authority could be potential victimizers of the vulnerable people she sought to protect and heal. They were to be approached warily and with distrust.

These patterns, rooted in her spiritual agreement "to care for the vulnerable," got her into a lot of trouble with well-meaning caring authorities. People grew tired of her suspicion and paranoia in reaction to what appeared to them to be simple requests of her connected to the jobs she held as teacher and chaplain.

Valerie, whose mother died suddenly, had several patterns of interaction that posed obstacles to working through her grief. The theological principle that she struggled with was that "good religious people do not feel anger toward those they love and honor." She had learned that anger was something to be pushed aside. It was destructive to express it or to share it with others.

Janet, the woman who collected illnesses, claimed that her problems were the responsibility of others, even while she requested the help of others. She would relay her great litany of problems and constantly react as a victim with her relatives and friends, playing "one up" with them whenever they had problems or illnesses. She wanted success and achievement but was blocked by blaming others for life's challenges.

I said earlier that *who we are for people* is the most important gift we have to offer. Its impact is felt whether it carries negative connotations or positive ones. Spiritual caregivers often think that people only respond to their words or their overt actions. But people in crisis are keenly aware of nuances in relationships. They look for engagement and acceptance or a lack thereof.

If the spiritual caregiver feels sorry for the person receiving care, that person will pick it up quickly, especially if they are in crisis. If the caregiver sees the person as a victim with few resources to draw upon, the person will feel that their ability to cope with the situation is being diminished.

Very often people are a mass of contradictions when they relate to a spiritual caregiver. They may want to please, fear to share, feel guilty, or respond to some innate trust in the role by believing the caregiver may have some answers for life's questions or solutions to life's conflicts. All of these and more may be triggered in the development of the relationship. The spiritual caregiver needs to create a space where these reactions can be tested, questions asked, and conflicts worked through.

Henri Nouwen in his book *Reaching Out* says:

> In our world full of strangers, estranged from our past, culture and country from their neighbors, friends and family; from their deepest self and their God, we witness

a painful search for a hospitable place where life can be
lived without fear and where community can be found
. . . it is possible for men and women and obligatory for
spiritually committed people to offer an open and hospitable space where strangers can cast off their strangeness
and become our fellow human beings.[1]

1. Nouwen, *Reaching Out*, 46.

13

Spiritual Agreements with the Holy

WHETHER PEOPLE ARE RELIGIOUS or spiritual, with or without faith, life principles and values grow exponentially in influence when we apply spirituality to them. Spiritual agreements or covenants develop early in our lives and are often based on unexplored, unyielding religious or spiritual principles. Many life decisions arise from these principles. The roots of the covenants are in the family relationships that helped to form our images of the Holy or what is perceived to be holy. Agreements are most often formed not out of free choice or grace but out of fear of certain punishments or reprisals that hold significant power.

These kinds of agreements limit our ability to bring healthy religious resources to cope with a crisis. The covenants carry not only religious or spiritual resources that help us manage crises, but they also carry negative influences that cripple our ability to live in abundance. For example, a covenant that implies we must be successful to earn the Divine's favor may bring us achievement in the business world but may limit the freedom we feel in our relationships.

Spiritual caregivers need to look at their own covenants to see if they are congruent with what they preach and believe to be true about themselves and their relationships. This examination becomes vitally important if we are to help others do the same. The elements of these personal covenants with God are:

a. family history and system that help form the covenant,

b. a lifelong prayer that captures the agreement in a prayer-phrase,

c. personal behavior that would break our prayer-phrase,

d. and an agreement that is formed to avoid the "personal unforgivable sin" or the agreement breaker above.

The following are examples of covenants of spiritual caregivers with whom I've worked.

Martha

a. Family history: Martha was the oldest in a large family. There was no time to waste being sad or crying; there was always too much to do. Her father was strong, aloof, non-touching. He was rarely pleased and gave little praise.

b. Prayer: "Oh Lord, let me be pleasing to you." When asked how pleasing looked, Martha responded, "To be competent, hardworking, together, and resourceful."

c. Agreement breaker: To appear to be unpleasing, vulnerable, weak, uncertain, lazy, incompetent.

d. Agreement: "I am your person as long as I am, or least appear to be, competent, hardworking, together."

e. Impact on relationships: Martha felt affirmation from God when she worked hard. The emphasis was on doing rather than being. She clearly felt that weakness, fear, and anger were unacceptable to God. At one point, when she was feeling down and angry, she talked about feeling abandoned by God. She spoke often of grace but did not apply it to her relationship with God. Behind her competent exterior was her anger;

her worldview was "it's your fault" (why didn't you love all of me?), and her belief was that "I don't need to change." Martha was an Achiever. The primary dis-ease was in her need to be responsible and reconciled.

James

a. Family history: James had a father who was weak and ineffectual yet controlling. James received support during crises, struggles, fears, and uncertainty but not for accomplishments. In times of illness or crisis his mother was especially attentive.

b. Prayer: "Lord, you are my strength."

c. Agreement breaker: To be or appear strong, competent, resourceful. This was experienced as a denial of the Divine's strength in his life. He was threatened when encouraged to act from strengths, to formulate care plans, and draw on his considerable resources in his spiritual care.

d. Agreement: "I am your person as long as I give you the credit and as long as I am one of the meek and the weak."

e. Impact on relationships: The Divine seemed distant yet overpowering. To stay right with his spiritual agreement meant he assumed a humble, meek stance. His self-view was "I can't change" (that's the way I am, and I am valued in my weakness and vulnerability). His worldview was "I am at fault." James was a Giver with many gifts for caring for others. The primary dis-ease in his need was in his self-worth.

James paid a high price for his covenant. He was forced to suppress a bright, quick mind and sensitivity. His gifts lacked focus and direction because his covenant constantly forced him to squelch his gifts.

Mateo

a. Family history: Mateo was the oldest child in a family that had lost their father when the children were young. His mother was often depressed and at times suicidal. This left Mateo with fears that life could be tenuous, uncertain, and short.

b. Prayer: "Lord, let me sample all that life has for me."

c. Agreement breaker: To miss out on opportunities.

d. Agreement: "I am your person as long as I taste all of what God has for me."

e. Impact on relationships: Mateo was caring, creative, and capable. However, while he started many projects and programs and had good ability for them, he rarely finished. He often had a "full plate" and could be distracted by opportunities. Mateo was a Searcher and the dis-ease he experienced was in commitment.

These covenants exercise considerable power in people's lives. People risk a great deal in changing them. Someone trying to change them may experience a feeling of dying. Changing may mean committing the covenant or agreement breaker to feel free from the rigidity of the agreement. It may require a drastic change in the way people behave in relationships. The spiritual care provider's role is to create an environment in which these risks can be taken, agreements changed, and new life claimed.

This was James's experience once he made the decision to appreciate and act out of his strengths. This move came at considerable spiritual and emotional expense. It caused him to change several theological tenants in his definition of humility in Christian life. He needed to restructure relationships with friends who had given him support and sympathy during his struggles. It meant being the initiator at times rather than the reactor. In short, changing that covenant meant restructuring his inner and outer world. It was not easy for James, but each step brought new life and greater freedom in his relationship with the Divine and with others.

If a spiritual caregiver hears a person's prayer and can identify it as a long-held prayer, they should know with some certainty the person's agreement breaker and covenant. Martha shared her prayer as "Oh Lord, let me be pleasing to you." Pleasing meant "hardworking and together." It was not a great leap to assume her "breaker" was to be lazy or not together and to assume that she came from a family that was demanding and put a high premium on success and hard work. This is not a mysterious ability nor does it take a great amount of time. It does take some experience with hearing people's stories, knowing similarities between images of the Holy and relationships with families of origin.

Knowing Martha's agreement breaker and covenant directed my response as I tried to care for her. Her silent cry of "Why did you not love all of me?" directed to her parents was the key phrase.

I needed to embody someone who could love all of her and could allow her to "feel," especially anger, in our relationship. She was stuck in the ritual process at the point of judgment. She needed to be able to get angry and blame her parents before she could realize her responsibility for her own situation. I could be a person who could help her to do that by allowing it to happen in our relationship.

The responsibility, which she needed to accept, was the distance she created in relationships by withholding and denying her feelings. She did not have a clear picture of who she was, particularly when she was angry.

My relationship with James improved after I had begun to be community for him in a new way. He needed a new community in which he could be strong. My most important contribution to him was to be intuitive and sensitive with him yet still be strong and structured. I began to share my own feelings and fears and my own intuitions. I allowed my artistic side to become a part of our relationship, and I tried to demonstrate that strength and sensitivity could coexist in one person.

With Mateo I was clearly the "caller" to decision and commitment. He came very close to finishing the certification program I was leading, but he suddenly announced that he had to move on.

Being in one place and putting down roots was hard for him. Life and commitment could not be trusted.

Going back to previous examples, with Jack, covenants became important in understanding him. When the priest caring for him assessed his core need as self-worth and asked him what he would pray for if he ever prayed, his answer came quickly: "Strength, I'd pray for strength, man, to put up with all this. I would not show these turkeys they could get to me."

Jack did not believe he was strong. His behavior was rooted in his fear that he was weak. When he began to reveal his feelings, his fear and lack of self-worth emerged. Calling him to share his sensitivities put him in violation of the way he had structured his life. The priest, who grew to care for him, incarnated and embodied a sensitive, strong man and attempted to create a new community for him.

The woman who collected diseases, Janet, was very angry with God for the hardship in her life, but her covenant prevented her from getting angry and blaming God. The more the minister probed those feelings, the more defensive the woman became.

Being angry at God and showing her lack of gratitude was against her conservative upbringing. She was stuck in the ritual process at judgment. Before she could take responsibility for her life, she needed to get angry and blame. She was being called in that situation to change her understandings of theology and her covenant with the Holy.

Gloria, the forty-two-year-old woman who panicked while driving a car, most likely had a spiritual agreement breaker of acting for her own sake or "selfishly." Making decisions that were for her and not for her family threatened her. It was the task of the caregiver to create a community for her in which she could take such risks, still be accepted, and continue to grow.

The middle-aged architect, John, who was struggling with meaning and direction, was trying to live by his family of origin rules to care for the family by being a good provider. When the architect's new vocation threatened these principles, he felt lost.

Finding new meaning and purpose put him at risk with his agreement breaker: "to risk becoming an inadequate provider for his family." The caregiver's task was to call him to the new meaning in the face of those risks.

Covenants or spiritual agreements are guardians of needs. They determine in large measure a person's type and ability to bring healthy religious or spiritual resources to cope with crises. The spiritual care provider needs to create an environment in which people experience care, care that fosters enough courage to risk changing their spiritual agreements with the Holy.

Below is a diagram that shows the relationship between types, needs, and spiritual agreements.

Type	Need	Ritual	Spiritual Agreement
Achiever	Responsibility	Reconciliation	"As long as I succeed and achieve, I am right with the Holy"
Giver	Worth	Community	"As long as I care for others, I am right with the Holy"
Searcher	Commitment	Vocation	"As long as I am open to all opportunities, I am right with the Holy"

Summary

It is a new day for spiritual care. The impact of this care is being studied, valued, and published like never before. This means that what we do, how we do it, and how we gauge outcomes become vitally important.

Spiritual care providers need to believe that what we do and who we are for people heal and enrich life. When theological and spiritual views have negative impact, we need to be able to identify, reform, or reeducate in order to bring resources that will enhance people's lives.

We need to have a system that helps us assess people using our language. We need to respond to people with a care plan and be able to articulate outcomes. In that sense we need a standard of practice.

By now, I hope you have seen how spiritual caregivers can do this and can contribute to language that can be shared with others in a professional environment.

Spiritual care response is informed by spiritual care assessment. It is in line with theological and spiritual covenants. It is both embodied care and service.

It is as important for ministers to know themselves before the Holy and within themselves as to know the people whom they serve. The previous framework is intended to give caregivers direction to set goals, to have some sense when goals are achieved, and to be as fully informed as possible in bringing the presence of the Divine to others. Those are the principles that are needed to break the code for spiritual care and establish a standard of practice.

14

History and Curiosity

I'VE OFTEN THOUGHT ABOUT the characteristics of the type of person who is best suited for spiritual care. Some, like caring or trustworthiness, are important, but one close to the top of the list for me is curiosity. If you're not curious about the people you're caring for or about yourself, spiritual care is limited. Engage with people to show your interest, discover, and help them discover.

Some spiritual caregivers don't see the value in knowing one's own history or the history of the person to whom care is offered. The reasons most often given are that it is not their job to involve themselves in people's history or they simply don't have the time. A third reason is that they don't know what to do with it. It is possible to gather information about personal history very quickly. This preliminary work saves time and frustration because *it is history* that creates types and forms needs and spiritual agreements.

People can change some of their overt behaviors and yet retain the same underlying motivations and feelings formed in their history.

A lay woman, whom I met at a seminar on spiritual care and who was a parish visitor in training, is an illustration of this point. I had been talking with the group about the importance of assessment and history and how it formed spiritual agreements. During a break she told me that she had been in therapy for many years and suffered from eating disorders, principally bulimia. She had been counseled by her pastor and had been in eating disorder support groups. The pastor had also done some marriage counseling with her and her husband because of "the strain her problems had put on her marriage." She said, "I've never told anybody this, but I was sexually abused by my father as a child. No one has ever asked me if there was sexual abuse in my history, but it has defined me. They kept trying to help me with what they saw as my main problem." This is a dramatic story, but it illustrates the point that significant time and effort can be wasted if personal history does not get appropriate attention. Wandering through personal histories with no aim or goal is frivolous at best, voyeuristic or abusive at worst, and not helpful. Entering people's histories for the purpose of isolating life principles and spiritual commitments that created their strengths, limitations, and need areas has significant purpose.

There are times when changes being suggested may not seem difficult to the caregiver but are felt as monumental by the care receiver because of history and the spiritual nature of what is being changed. For people to change basic agreements or covenants, they need to be able to understand those changes in theological or spiritual terms as well as the process for changing.

Unexamined rigid spiritual principles lead to weak spots in people's need areas and coping resources. They become places where dis-ease is most likely to occur. Therefore, the unexamined, unyielding spiritual principles offer caregivers information about the places where people are most likely to get stuck in the ritual process. They may tell us what to embody for people as we care for them. Understanding these principles will enable the spiritual caregiver to be able to speak directly to the root cause of dis-ease and help persons enter a process in which they can examine these commitments and choose more abundant living.

It is important to look at key environmental factors that contribute to people's patterns, assessing the significant relationships in families of origin, whether persons were loved or beaten, whether they had family or friends who could be trusted. All of this gives information about their basic stances in life and how they were formed.

Being a woman and or a person of color in our society is a different experience than being a white male. Being from a poor family or a middle-income or upper-income family contributes to the formation of personal identity and basic life values.

Sarah, the minister who refused to hurt others, was sexually abused as a child. Martha was the oldest in a very large family in which very little affirmation was given to her and her siblings. James, on the other hand, received too much affirmation at the wrong times. Jack grew up in a series of foster homes, never really knew his parents, and received very little love or appropriate discipline.

Out of these kinds of histories we begin to form worldviews that define for us our basic approaches to life events. Out of these circumstances come the beliefs: "I am at fault," "You are at fault," or "I am lost."

Martha learned to be tough, a leader, and to deny her own feelings and the feelings of others. Sarah learned not to trust; she learned to protect herself emotionally from further disappointment and abuse by setting herself up in an adversarial relationship with anyone who might threaten her. Jack was deficient in his ability to love or take responsibility.

Out of our historical internal reactions, our primary type is formed, our needs get expressed, and our spiritual agreements with the Divine become the guardians of our lives.

This does not mean that ministers need to be the major caregivers in every situation. There are times to choose not to be that caregiver. The next section of this book talks about spiritual referral. It is important to point out that deciding that a person's struggles are beyond the spiritual caregiver's abilities does not mean she or he ought not do the assessment or response. It does infer that whether the caregiver is the main caregiver or not there is still spiritual care needed. This includes translating the situation and the needs into spiritual or theological terms.

Section 2: Spiritual Care Response

The spiritual care provider's abilities to theologize or spiritualize their care and help the person receiving the care do the same remains a primary ingredient in choosing new life.

SECTION 3

Spiritual Care Referral

I HAVE SEEN LITTLE written about spiritual care referral. The only book I've seen on the topic is *Referral in Pastoral Counseling* by William Oglesby, written many years ago. This was an important book for me because it did not use criteria that we often see today. In the book, referral was not based on topics that the spiritual caregiver should not deal with, but it gave a structure for understanding time limitations, experience, and the like.

When I worked in a large religious-based hospital in the Midwest, the point was brought home to me. I happened to be sitting in the office of the director of pastoral care, who was an older nun. She received a phone call from a psychiatrist who had a "complaint about one of her chaplains." The psychiatrist did more than lodge the complaint; he gave an ultimatum. His first mistake. He said that the chaplain had been talking about sex with a patient and that was totally unacceptable and not appropriate for a chaplain to do and he did not want it to happen again. There was a significant pause in the conversation until the director said, "Doctor, I have known you for a very long time. I was your principal when you were in high school. I was here at the hospital when you were a psychiatric resident. I cannot think of a person less qualified to talk about sex with a patient than you. I am open to hearing from you on how my chaplains are doing but don't ever tell me what my chaplains can or can't do."

There are several morals to that story. The first is, probably, don't mess with a nun. The second is that there are criteria in deciding who should be talking about what with patients, but it has little to do with the topic of the conversation or the inherent role of the caregiver.

There is a difference between spiritual caregivers who refer and a spiritual care referral. The pattern for many is that they base their decisions regarding referral on the issues of the person receiving care. They tend to discount the value of an ongoing role in the continued care of the person and step away after the referral. It seems as if once a particular issue is determined to be beyond the spiritual caregiver, she or he gives up responsibilities for either spiritual care assessment or response in the situation. However, the responsibilities to be a diacritic, to make an assessment and plan a response and make it part of the overall care plan, continues after a referral is made.

There are two major factors in referral. The first is the preference of the person receiving care. I believe in a system of care that places the person at the center of decision making regarding their health. The person should have freedom for deciding the team members who are involved in their care.

The second set of factors include a realistic assessment of the issues and the skills of the spiritual caregiver. I have seen several books that talk about the criteria for referring to spiritual care. I have only seen the Oglesby book speak to criteria for the spiritual caregiver referring.

15

Criteria for Referrals and How to Refer

THE CRITERIA OGLESBY OUTLINES in his book are helpful for spiritual caregivers when knowing how to refer.

a. Time limitations—Oglesby notes that the spiritual caregiver may have the skill and experience to deal with the problem presented but may not have the time. For a congregational minister or a professional in a hospital, long-term spiritual care and the time it requires may not match the priorities of the role.

b. Skill or experience limitation—The primary consideration in this area is that the person receiving care is describing a situation or feeling that seems not coherent or logical to the spiritual caregiver. The issue transcends the personal experience of the caregiver.

c. Emotional security limitation—There are several factors involved here, including that the presenting issue is one that the caregiver has not resolved in his or her life or that the issue being struggled with is so much like the caregiver's issues that there is little objectivity.

This situation may be most difficult for the caregiver to refer. When caregivers are most involved in other's emotions and most unclear of their own emotional involvement, they are less likely to refer.

   d. Personal knowledge of self limitations—It is important that the spiritual caregiver has done an inventory of their own relationship with the Divine and has enough self-knowledge of their history and needs to provide care in an effective manner.[1]

How to Refer

a. The first principle of referring is to *focus on the person* receiving the care and on their issues. This balances the over dependence of a specific caregiver being the only one able to help with this person's unique problems. The spiritual caregiver can help the person understand their issues theologically or spiritually whether they are the primary caregiver or not.

   In our clinic at the Institute for Health and Healing, a woman was being cared for by several people. She met with our MD nutritionist, a body worker, our psychotherapist, and me as her spiritual caregiver. I worked with her as she sought to make her ideas and relationship with God healthier. She had several psychological concerns, and I referred her to the psychotherapist to get more consistent counseling care than I could provide. She did come to me periodically to check in and place her growing insights into harmony with her relationship with God. This was a good example of teamwork and how spiritual care continued to help after a referral.

b. The second principle is to work toward *helping the person feel that the referral is not a rejection.* If the spiritual caregiver has some clear ideas of what their limitations of time or issues might be, then that ought to be shared in the early part of the relationship. A decision to refer will then be less likely to be seen as rejection. The woman above felt that she was being cared for by

1. Oglesby, *Referral in Pastoral Counseling*, 36.

a team so that my referral was easier for her to handle. It also helped that she could come to me as her treatment progressed.

c. The third principle is that the referral should *always involve the participation of the person receiving the care.* The person needs to be involved in the decision to seek further help as much as possible. I talked to the woman before I made my referral. She had begun to talk about serious family issues in her youth. She agreed that the issues needed consistent attention. I talked to her about how the pain she felt then influenced her images of God as one who punished and judged. We agreed to continue to talk as she worked with other team members.

d. The fourth principle is that *help is seen as an addition to, rather than in place of, the spiritual care.* If the spiritual caregiver sees themself as having responsibility for assessment and response, then the person receiving care is more likely to understand this principle. The spiritual caregiver can still be community, an avenue for reconciliation and direction. This involvement helps other care be put in the context of the person's faith framework.

e. The fifth principle is that *the spiritual caregiver relates beyond referral* when that is possible.

There are other disciplines and uncommissioned lay people that believe that they do spiritual care. They do. It is important that they also use the criteria above to refer to the professional spiritual caregiver. Throughout this book I have detailed the skills and insight it takes to be a responsible caregiver. It can be a complex undertaking and, while there are roles that others can contribute, the contributions should be given respecting the depth of the field.

When I was a young minister interning in a congregation on the East Coast, I set up a small group-sharing experience with women in the congregation. This was with the permission of the supervising pastor and was part of the research connected to my doctorate. Each of the participants agreed to be part of the study and the group. I learned two things very quickly. The first was that the support group for these women, who primarily worked in the home, was needed and appreciated. The second was that I was over my head and was hearing some material that I had not dealt with or been trained for. With some help from my supervising pastor and my advisor in the degree program, I began to sort through what I could handle and what I couldn't. I referred two of the women who wanted individual attention to a trusted therapist in the community. They remained in the support group and we continued to work at attaching faith and spiritual principles to the issues that were being dealt with.

While that group was a long time ago, the principles listed in Oglesby's book have helped me each step of the way throughout my spiritual care career. There have always been times when I have not had the experience or training or needed objective distance to help people in the most effective way. Most of those times, when I was not the primary caregiver, I was able to contribute to helping people bring their faith resources to bear in their situations.

Conclusion

PROFESSIONAL SPIRITUAL CARE IS one of the most difficult professional occupations. There are very few guidelines for how to do the job, which makes evaluating it difficult. At the same time, there are an amazing number of expectations. Spiritual caregiving is very broadly defined and occurs in a wide variety of situations. Burnout is high as caregivers search for ways to deal with the expectations within themselves and from others.

If this book has helped the spiritual caregiver become clearer about their role in the care, given some ideas of how to judge when goals are reached, and moved toward a standard of practice for the field, then it has made a significant contribution.

The one who speaks for the community to the Holy has been with us since the beginning of time. There was a period in the twentieth century when certain groups of spiritual caregivers gave up using spiritual or theological language in work with people. It is time for us to reclaim our spot of prominence in caring for people. The people that have been cared for over the years have never lost sight of the fact that we are important to them. We need to be faithful to the trust people have placed in us.

While church membership wanes, the need to connect to the Holy, especially in crisis, does not.

It is again time for those of us who have been set apart from our communities to be faithful to the call to preach good news to the poor, free the captives, be prophets to people and systems who need to hear prophetic words, and be caregivers who will believe enough in the Divine and in themselves to speak with courage to people in the midst of crises.

I have presented structures for understanding and evaluating spiritual care. I am also aware that what we and other helping professions do is an art born of who we are and what we hold dear. At the same time, I hope that this book has contributed to the science of understanding the theological and spiritual needs of people for whom we care. Spiritual care is not nebulous. It is proactive and structured and can be communicated, charted, and evaluated.

I am convinced that our abilities and the resources we have available to us are clearly sufficient for us to be good diacritics, good assessors of people's situations and their lives. Our resource bank is at least as full as the other professions. The call for this age is that we begin to use those resources in a way that respects our ability to be healers, that causes us to communicate more precisely what we do, and sends us out to research and write.

Bibliography

Arrien, Angeles. *The Four-Fold Way*. New York: HarperCollins, 2013.

Best, Megan, et al. "An EAPC White Paper on Multi-Disciplinary Education for Spiritual Care in Palliative Care." *BMC Palliative Care* 19 (2020) 9.

———. "A Long Way to Go Understanding the Role of Chaplaincy? A Critical Reflection on the Findings of the Survey Examining Chaplaincy Responses to Covid-19." *Journal of Pastoral Care & Counseling* 75 (2021) 46–48.

Beverly, Urias. *Spiritual Alignment: From God to Eternity*. New York: Page, 2019.

Cadge, Wendy. *Spiritual Care: The Everyday Work of Chaplains*. New York: Oxford University Press, 2023.

Capps, Donald. *Pastoral Care: A Thematic Approach*. Eugene, OR: Wipf & Stock, 2003.

Clevenger, Casey, et al. "Education for Professional Chaplaincy in the US: Mapping Current Practice in Clinical Pastoral Education (CPE)." *Health Care Chaplaincy* 27 (2021) 222–37.

Clinebell, Howard. *Basic Types of Pastoral Care and Counseling*. Nashville: Abingdon, 2011.

Doehring, Carrie. *The Practice of Pastoral Care*. Rev. ed. Louisville: Westminster John Knox, 2015.

Duffy, Regis. *Real Presence*. Eugene, OR: Wipf & Stock, 2010.

Kegan, Robert, et al. *Toward Moral and Religious Maturity*. New York: Silver Burdette, 1980.

Kenny, Dennis. *Book of Weeks: A Guide for Transformational Education*. Lulu, 2005.

———. *Promise of the Soul: Identifying and Healing Your Spiritual Agreements*. New York: Wiley, 2002.

Koenig, Harold. *Spirituality in Patient Care*. West Conshohocken, PA: Templeton, 2013.

LeShan, Lawrence. *Landscapes of the Mind*. Guilford, CT: Eirini, 2013.

———. *The Mechanic and the Gardener*. Ballwin, MO: Holt, Rinehart, and Winston, 1982.

Mounce, William. *Analytical Lexicon*. Grand Rapids: Zondervan Academic, 1993.

Bibliography

Nouwen, Henri. *Reaching Out*. Grand Rapids: Zondervan, 1998.

O'Donohue, John. *Eternal Echoes*. New York: Harper Perennial, 2000.

Oglesby, William, Jr. *Referral in Pastoral Counseling*. Englewood Cliffs, NJ: Prentice-Hall 1968.

Palmer, Parker. *The Courage to Teach*. New York: Wiley, 2009.

———. *Let Your Life Speak*. San Francisco: Jossey-Bass, 2000.

Pargament, Kenneth. *Spiritually Integrated Psychotherapy*. New York: Guilford, 2011.

Pargament, Kenneth, et al. "The Brief RCOPE: Current Psychometric Status of a Short Measure of Religious Coping." *Religions* 2 (2020) 51–76.

Pruyser, Paul. *The Minister as Diagnostician*. Louisville: Westminster, 1976.

Rahe, Richard H., et al. "The Stress and Coping Inventory: An Educational and Research Instrument." *Stress & Health* 16 (2000) 199–208.

Seymour, Ruth. "Clergy and Stress." *Detroit Free Press*. Sunday, January 5, 1986.

Wimberly, Edward. *African American Pastoral Care*. Rev. ed. Nashville: Abingdon, 2010.

Wise, Carroll. *The Meaning of Pastoral Care*. New York: Harper & Row, 1966.

Index

Index

Index

Made in the USA
Columbia, SC
30 October 2023

25212397R00083